Tuscan Escapes

Tuscan Escapes

inspirational homes in Tuscany and Umbria

CAROLINE CLIFTON-MOGG

photography by Chris Tubbs

RYLAND
PETERS
& SMALL

LONDON NEW YORK

SENIOR DESIGNER Isabel de Cordova
SENIOR EDITOR Henrietta Heald
LOCATION RESEARCH Emily Westlake
PRODUCTION Sheila Smith
ART DIRECTOR Anne-Marie Bulat
PUBLISHING DIRECTOR Alison Starling

First published in the UK in 2006 by
Ryland Peters & Small
20–21 Jockey's Fields
London WC1R 4BW
www.rylandpeters.com

10 9 8 7 6 5 4 3 2 1

ISBN-10: 1-84597-243-0
ISBN-13: 978-1-84597-243-1

A CIP record for this book is available from
the British Library.

Printed and bound in China.

contents

introduction

Like all the world's most romantic places, Tuscany is a state of mind as well as a physical entity. Say the T-word to Tuscophiles and their eyes take on a faraway look, as if they have suddenly been transported to that landscape, those houses, this village – all bathed in the bright, clear Tuscan light that has inspired so much great art over the centuries. This artistic heritage is particularly associated with the period of the Italian Renaissance, when, in cities such as Florence and Siena, painters, sculptors, architects – Giotto, Raphael, Botticelli, Leonardo, Donatello, Michelangelo, Brunelleschi – created works of art that have influenced and informed European culture for more than 500 years.

Indeed, for many foreigners to the region, Renaissance Italy *is* Tuscany – which may explain why the Tuscan landscape seems so strange and yet so familiar: the rounded hills dotted with tall, cigar-shaped cypresses and olive groves, the rambling stone buildings and bell towers, and the dusty narrow roads along which one would hardly be surprised to see a cavalcade of noble horsemen, in plumed hats and gold-embroidered tunics, clattering up the hill on their way to hunt wild deer and boar. Artists working in Siena, Florence, Arezzo and other Tuscan towns composed their religious and secular works against a background made up of local landmarks – hills, trees and orchards, vineyards and olive groves, monasteries and churches – which is why, even more than in the rest of Italy, Tuscany is a place where the past, both recent and distant, is always present.

For centuries Tuscany was farming country, attested to by the large number of farmsteads that are still there today; but over the years many left the land to look for city work, leaving some farms forgotten, others derelict, some in ruins. These are the buildings now being bought by Tuscany lovers, foreign or native. The houses range from the utterly simple – a one-room dwelling originally shared with farm animals – to the grand and imposing – often more a fortified manor than a farmhouse.

Whether large or small, most Tuscan farmhouses were architecturally concerned with different priorities from those of our own day. Rather than encouraging the sun into every corner and crevice, most of these homesteads were built to keep the weather out – in summer to maintain a cool, soothing escape from the heat, and in winter to keep the often icy winter at bay through thick walls and small window openings. One of the interesting aspects of *Tuscan Escapes* is how our different home owners have creatively modified the Tuscan original to suit the needs and desires of the 21st century.

In many parts of Tuscany, as elsewhere in Europe, the conversion or restoration of a house can take place only within strict planning constraints; often the converted house may not extend beyond the bounds of the original, and changes must be made within the original foundations or 'footprint' of the existing building. The extent to which ingenuity and imaginative design flourishes under these conditions is well illustrated by the houses on these pages, for in *Tuscan Escapes* there are examples of homes from the smallest to the largest, and in every style. Some are in villages, some isolated; some are extremely old, others not so. Some were almost industrial buildings; some have been inhabited for hundreds of years. All are different, yet all share that ineffable sense of comfort, style and, above all, well-being that we have come to associate with the many rich pleasures of Tuscan life.

natural
charm

In many ways, Tuscan life has remained unchanged for centuries. Values and standards persist, especially regarding the use of natural materials and traditional crafts. Italy has always been the home of craftsmen. In places such as Florence and Venice, leather workers, jewellers, bookbinders and silversmiths still work in studios all over the city, and in many parts of the countryside first-class artisans — cabinetmakers, ironworkers, painters — are plentiful. These links with tradition emphasize the ever-present sense in Tuscany of being close to, even part of, the land. Unsurprisingly, there is little that is not natural in the rural Tuscan home. The colours — ochres, umbers, warm reds — are earth colours; the textiles are the most natural of weaves; building materials are those that have always been used — wood, iron, terracotta; and even the production of various elements from woodwork to floor tiles follows well-tried design principles.

For much of the year, living and eating outside is a priority. Everything flows naturally outwards — the immediate garden and terraces, the trees beyond and the surrounding landscape are as important a part of the whole as the kitchen or bedroom. It is no wonder, therefore, that natural charm is the order of the day.

earthy paradise

When it comes to the restoration of old houses, particularly old Tuscan farmhouses, there is always a style conundrum to resolve. Should the house be brought smartly into the 21st century or treated as a contemporary example of an older, earthier time? The owners of this house chose the latter route.

La Lite – the Tuscan home of Toia Saibene, her sister Giuliana and Giuliana's husband Federico Magnifico – is an old, partly restored farmhouse near Lucignano. They bought the house in 1979 from the Marchese Lotaringi della Stufa, who still lives in the nearby Castello del Calcione, which itself dates from 1483.

Traditionally, La Lite had been inhabited by peasant families who cultivated the land for themselves and gave a share of the produce to the landlord in return. This was part of a system that had been established several hundred years previously – the earliest part of the house dates from the 17th century – and over the years the land had been used for the cultivation of olive

Opposite The family has been careful to furnish the house simply and with suitably rustic furniture. This corner of the living room is distinguished by a local Tuscan desk and a quirky, woven-seated childbirth chair also found locally.

Left A country bench with its integral storage chest is the centrepiece of a rustic tableau incorporating everything around it, from the sabots on the floor to the decorative straw hats on the wall and the hand-made baskets on the seat.

trees, vines, wheat and mulberry trees for silkworms. When Toia and her family first saw the house, it had been abandoned for 20 years and needed a great deal of work to transform it into a habitable dwelling. Their intention was to return the house to its original look and character – that of a peasants' house on a working estate. There was also a large amount of reconstruction to be done outside: since the house had been neglected for so long, it was necessary to re-establish the plantation of olive trees and also to allow the land to recuperate.

Although doing the restoration in the right way was important to Toia and her family, they did not wish – as would few people today, no matter how committed to authenticity – to use the space in exactly the same way as it had been in earlier centuries. So it was no hardship that it was not possible to restore the living plan entirely to its original layout, which had allowed for family life on the first floor while the ground floor held the stables and pigsty as well as storage for farm machinery, utensils and some produce. Much basic work needed to be done: they replaced the

Right An ultra-rustic dormitory: three matching Tuscan beds with imposing raised headboards have been arranged beside matching Tuscan tables; narrow striped bedcovers add to the room's austere formality.

Opposite Toia's bedroom is a symphony of the colours of the countryside, from the terracotta floor tiles to the original red-brown shutters and the quilted bedcover. The bed, as so much else in the house, is Tuscan.

Below The forging of wrought-iron is a traditional skill in Tuscany, and this pair of beds exemplifies the simple charms of the art. The frames are set off by simple white bedcovers and an atmospheric lamp that resembles an old oil lamp.

roof, installed a heating system and rewired the property. They also put in two bathrooms. La Lite now consists of a living room, a large kitchen incorporating a dining area, and five bedrooms. Throughout the house Toia and her family have tried to use the original materials as far as they could and, fortunately, were able to keep the existing walls and floors and the original kitchen sink, as well as the large fireplace.

It is abundantly clear that the family has succeeded in its aims: each room looks as though it has merely been rescued from some ancient sleeping spell – there is no suggestion of the type of extensive work that had to be undertaken. This illusion is helped by the choice of furnishings and decorative processes. 'We have done what we could to maintain the original peasant style, choosing simple rustic furniture that we bought in the nearby village,' explains Toia.

The walls are plastered, using a finish known as *a calce*, which involves adding the colour directly to the plaster, and the windows are painted in a brick colour

'We have done what we could to maintain the original peasant style, choosing simple rustic furniture that we bought in the nearby villages.'

as they would have been originally. The fabrics used in the furnishing of the house are simple in design and found locally; the one exception is the room in which the family has used Indian fabrics bought on various travels.

Outside, the warm tones of the outer walls invite peace and quiet in the sun; these external walls are made in typical Tuscan style, which alternates stone and brick. They added a pergola, to provide the necessary shade in this often very hot part of the country, and a long table, which they found in a local church.

It is not as straightforward as it might appear to restore a house in the style in which it was originally designed while also making it functional. It is a testament to the trio that they have succeeded so well in capturing the best of traditional rural life while ensuring that beneath the timeless surface are all the essential underpinnings of modern life.

romantic renovation

Anyone thinking of converting an Italian stone ruin into a comfortable home has to be seriously determined. If, in addition, you hail from London, cannot speak Italian and are unexpectedly alone, the determination factor needs to rise to almost superhuman levels.

Step forward Penny Radford, the owner of what is now a most charming group of dwellings in northern Umbria, but which when she discovered them were uninhabitable. The 'romantic' ruins that she had fallen in love with had once been a small farmstead, with the remains of a farmhouse – which still had a roof, but little else – an old olive mill and a cottage.

'It was the usual story,' says Penny. 'I was in my early forties, working in marketing in London. I'd had enough, wanted to change my life, saw the ruins with this spectacular view, fell in love, sold up and moved here. Sadly, it also turned out to be the beginning of the end of my marriage.'

Undaunted, and partly because she had no option, she decided to stick with the project, both in converting the rubble-strewn site and in mastering, pretty quickly, the rudiments of working Italian, by enrolling on a language course at Perugia University. Obviously, it would not be possible to restore all the buildings in the group at the same time, so Penny decided to start with the main house and slowly move on from there. 'Actually, part of the main house had once been restored, hence

Above and top **Among the joys of Il Prato di Sotto are the local landscape and the magical views – both major factors in Penny Radford's decision to buy what was little more than a heap of ruins and bring them back to verdant life.**

Left **Although Il Prato has an air of historical permanency, Penny built it virtually from scratch. Everything in this part of the house is new, including the staircase and arched doorway; a 'footprint' of the old house was all she had to work on.**

the partial roof, but restored very badly; I had originally thought that I might be able to do a bit and then live in it – possibly make one apartment, and let out another; but I realized that would be in the future – originally there wasn't one room one could live in, never mind an apartment, and my most pressing concern was to make a couple of rooms habitable.' So, during that first winter, she endured makeshift accommodation, made basic improvements to the property and studied her verbs. Amazingly, by the end of the first year, she not only had somewhere to live but also another apartment that she could let out; she had also run out of money. But a small setback like that was not going to daunt the indomitable Penny; she decided to sell her remaining securities and, as she says, 'hang in there'.

Gradually the whole site began to take shape. As she finished the apartments, visitors came to rent them, which allowed her to pay first for the construction of the cottage and later the restoration of the old olive mill and the swimming pool. Five years on, phase one of Prato di Sotto was complete.

It was time to tackle the remaining original ruined farmhouse. The plan was for a house for two, with, on the ground floor, a large sitting room for entertaining, a small library/hall and a working kitchen with an Aga – vital in the cold Italian winter – and a dining room at one end. Upstairs there was to be one very large bedroom with fantastic views and a small dressing room leading to the bathroom complete with a

This page and opposite **It is hard to imagine that when Penny bought Il Prato di Sotto, there was almost nothing there – certainly no ceilings complete with old beams. This kitchen is comfortable, warm and practical, seemingly dusted with the layers of other generations' lives upon it. Neither Italian nor English, it combines elements of both – reclaimed-tile floors and, as well as an efficient cooking range, a traditional English Aga – essential for warmth in the often long winters – plus a traditional carpenter's bench. Beyond the main kitchen is a useful utility room where more modern practicalities such as refrigerators are situated.**

Left and above **The dominant feature of the airy, comfortable living room is the handsome fireplace, which is composed of different pieces of old stone, including a beautifully carved cornice. The unusual panels of colour flanking the fireplace are by Dorothy Hancock.**

Right **The dining hall, with another attractive old fireplace, has a 19th-century Umbrian dining table and straight-backed chairs covered in wide stripes.**

300-year-old stone sink, and a central studio above the kitchen. There was also to be another bedroom with its own outside entrance, a self-contained apartment, opening out onto the vegetable garden.

All this was constructed almost literally from nothing. 'The original, very old building on this site hadn't been touched for several centuries; there was only the outline of the original walls, which gave us the footprint of a long narrow room, and so we started from there.'

What can be seen today is really a complete reconstruction project, with some of the structural elements new, others, such as the flooring, reclaimed – and all looking perfectly in period.

Many of the ideas for the conversion and reconstruction came from Penny's builders. She was lucky. It is still unusual in Italy for a woman – and a foreigner to boot – to take on such major projects on her own. 'I had no idea how hard it would be to do things. You come to a country like this and it is a real culture shock. People often don't tell you the truth. Instead, they tell you what they think you want to hear; that's the Italian way. They don't phone and nothing is ever what it appears. The information is rarely accurate and neither are the estimates. But I got to know my builders and they helped immensely.'

She didn't employ the services of an architect, since she felt that she knew quite well enough what she wanted, and the

Above **Reclaimed and restored pieces are found in abundance. In this simple bathroom, the basin is in fact an 18th-century stone sink, backed by 20th-century tiles. Above it is a late 19th-century French mirror.**

Above right **The study is warm and comfortable, again a mix of Italian and English styles, with its patterned upholstered chairs and red-toned rug, heavy beams and tiled floor.**

Right **Penny's bedroom has spectacular views; curtains are almost unnecessary. To the right of the window hangs her collection of early 20th-century watercolours. The chest at the end of the bed is Italian and 16th century.**

finished version is extremely accomplished. The decoration is a combination of the rural and the formal—an interesting amalgam of English country style and Italian sophistication, with elements from other cultures and countries introduced to the mix. Penny is also fortunate in having come from an art school background, and the colours that she has used throughout the property reflect this. They may be warm and earthy, but with a subtlety that marks them out from many another restored house.

The furniture and furnishings are different too: Penny has always collected furniture, and she brought many of her pieces over with her from England, as well as judiciously buying some Italian pieces to suit the rustic setting. The result is much warmer and more comfortable than is often the case, with deep cushioned sofas, rich-patterned kelims and full curtains. Even her choice of art is individual, with pictures ranging from groups of 20th-century watercolours to the two striking red canvases on either side of the fireplace – Dorothy Hancock's colour field panels, each consisting of many carefully applied, rich layers of paint.

Now that Penny has completed this mammoth restoration task, you might imagine that she would be content to sit back and enjoy the beauty that she has created at Prato di Sotto, and encourage others to do likewise. But that would be far from the truth. Instead, she has set up a restoration business helping Britons and Americans to find and renovate properties in the area. She is presently restoring another ruin for a client. Thank goodness, some people never learn.

among the olives

The British owners of this once abandoned farmhouse have achieved that for which so many inhabitants of cooler climes yearn. They have discovered a house in a beautiful part of the Italian countryside, restored it, and now live in it for much of the year.

It was not as easy as it sounds. First there was the finding, then there was the doing. 'We had been renting a house in the Chianti Classico area, dreaming of finding our own property,' says one of the owners. 'We wanted to live close to a particular medieval abbey. In 1985 we found a farmhouse that had once belonged to the abbey – overlooking it and built on the end of a ridge, giving panoramas on three sides.' Unlike many houses in the area, it was uninhabited but not derelict.

As is the case with all abandoned farmhouses, there was much work to be done. For example, the ground floor was made up of the original cowsheds. There was no functioning water supply nor plumbing, and all the outbuildings were in a parlous state. The massive job of restoration began. Within two years the house was habitable, and work continued for a further three years after that because it was important to the couple to get the structure of the house right, to let it to speak for itself. This illustrates a big difference in the thinking behind the restoration of this farmhouse and that of many others similar in size and make-up. The owners of this house are self-confessed perfectionists, as well as purists, and will settle for nothing less than the best, in whatever form it might take, and no matter how long it might take – five years being to them a not unreasonable length of time to make sure that the house was exactly right in every aspect.

The result is an appealing four-bedroomed main house with a small guest house in an outbuilding. Architectural and structural triumphs include an archway leading into the kitchen, which was uncovered and restored with old stone steps, and a kitchen fireplace constructed from old door posts. On the floors upstairs are the original brick tiles, and downstairs, where once there was only dirt and rubble, hand-made terracotta tiles have been laid. The kitchen, with its new–old fireplace and solid table, is the very heart of the house, as was traditional in all farmhouses, and the bedrooms exude an air of simple comfort. The perfectionist approach is illustrated by their choice of furniture for the house. They started with little furniture

Below and below right **Original wooden beams, stone steps and a rediscovered archway are among the structural elements that define the ground floor of this restored farmhouse.**

Opposite **Like every other room in the house, the kitchen is furnished and decorated in almost minimalist style. The wooden table is, unusually, graced with a marble top and the imposing kitchen fireplace was made, in part, with old posts, found elsewhere.**

Above **The owners wanted to furnish the house simply and sympathetically; they designed the console table in the hall. Carefully chosen handmade terracotta tiles have been laid throughout, replacing the original dirt and rubble floor.**

The owners sought to emphasize the reassuring solidity and wonderful variety of the old house's architecture, believing that you should 'feel' the building around you as you walk through it.

other than the old kitchen table. Slowly, though, they began to buy other pieces – 'an eclectic mix', they call it, with a preponderance of local antiques; they even made some pieces themselves. Their taste is essentially minimalist: 'We would rather have a few well-chosen things than a mass of objects that fill up every nook and cranny.'

Colour, in its purely decorative sense, is almost incidental; lime whitewash is used on almost all the walls, with the exception of two bedrooms and a bathroom, which are painted in yellow ochre tones. The owners feel that the house's architectural

Above **Its simple stillness gives this room instant appeal. It may emanate from the old kitchen table or the traditional wooden chairs with their rush seats, or even from the old doors that hide from view the essentials of modern kitchen life.**

Right and inset **The owners relish the detail and charm of this elaborately painted antique cupboard with its panels of flower sprays, which they found locally. Their taste is essentially minimalist, however, so every piece like the painted cupboard is balanced by something else that is very simple – in this case, the modern divan bed and night table. The floor is also left bare, with no carpet or rug to detract from its natural state.**

Below **One of the joys of an old house is small niches, alcoves and spaces that can be usefully employed for new purposes.**

*Above and above right **On the other side of the house from the paved terrace – and invisible from inside – is a swimming pool edged with local stone, which overlooks yet another spectacular landscape.***

structure – the tones created by the light and shadow cast by the floors, walls and ceilings – creates its own colour scheme, to which there is no need to add. Outside, invisible from the house – and from just about anywhere else – lies the attractive swimming pool.

All around the pool and the house is a carefully nurtured landscape supporting more than 600 olive trees – something that the owners feel strongly about: 'If you live in an olive-producing area, you should celebrate it by surrounding yourself with these perennially beautiful and evocative trees.' The olives are indeed evocative of the land and history of Tuscany, conveying as they do an air of permanence and serenity, the sense of which – so often sought after, so difficult to achieve – permeates the gardens and rooms of this tranquil house.

ancient bastion

The old stone tower that forms the centrepiece of this country home is a striking and formidable presence in the midst of the Chianti countryside. The sturdy edifice was constructed in about 1200 as a defence post, with stables at ground level and living quarters above. And it is a reminder in these more manicured times of the wilder, harder life that was once the lot of those who lived in this part of Italy.

Nicoletta and Vanni Calamai are not the first people to have lived here – and nor, probably, will they be the last, but their tenure to date has lasted more than three decades. During that period they have worked hard to adapt and fashion the original tower, which now houses the bedrooms, and the surrounding buildings that had been added over the centuries into an individual and comfortable home, using wherever possible the original materials and structure of the rooms.

In the past, long before the Calamais moved in, the building had been occupied by farmworkers before being abandoned for 20 years.

Above **Vanni Calamai, known for his handiwork in the house, made the wooden surround to the stone sink, which doubles as a handsome container.**

Right **The large kitchen fireplace has been set up as it might have been centuries ago, with a well-used cooking pot hanging from a trivet above the fire.**

The gradual restoration is continuing. 'I like moving things and decorating, and I like messing around with furniture and flowers,' says Nicoletta. The result does not look 'messed around', of course; it looks extremely cosy, and as if it had always been the way it is today. This is deliberate, since neither Nicoletta nor Vanni like the idea of modern fittings in an ancient house. For example, the kitchen, which leads off a conservatory entrance, is studiously low-key, with fittings hidden from sight. Once the stables, it now has the appearance of a comfortable living room.

Above **Under a set of stairs built by the farmers who once lived in the house, the Calamais have cleverly constructed a study area where once there was a very basic kitchen. A painted dado line divides the wall into separate areas of colour, picked up by the tones of the paintings on the wall and easel by artist Christine Szabo.**

Left **Enclosed by roughly hewn stone walls, this haphazardly charming area of the house now serves as part conservatory and part kitchen entrance.**

Above **When is a bathroom an unconventional bathroom – or even no bathroom at all? Answer: when it is simply a cosy corner in an otherwise traditionally furnished room.**

Above right **In the main bedroom, an old English commode chair has been granted a new lease of life as a desk chair – a perfect partner for the late 19th-century wooden bureau.**

Opposite **With its 200-year-old terracotta floor and its original vaulted ceiling, the main bedroom is a charming place, made more so by the traditional Tuscan iron bed married with an 18th-century Venetian mirror above the bedside table.**

'In these country houses, the kitchen is the first room you step into,' explains Nicoletta. 'So we didn't want it to be too kitchen-y in appearance; it had to be comfortable too. It's the room with the fireplace and where we have breakfast, lunch and dinner when we are not outside – and that's six months of the year. It is also the living room (with a television set hidden in the fireplace).' Many of the fittings – such as the slatted wooden chairs around the table, the wooden worktop with its inset sink – were made by Vanni Calamai, a self-confessed DIY enthusiast who likes nothing better than to work with wood, old and new. 'He adores fixing old objects and making them work,' says Nicoletta.

The bathroom creates a similar impression to the kitchen. It is a comfortable room that happens to be, by chance, somewhere you can have a bath. As Nicoletta says, 'In the old country houses there was no bathroom – just a "hanging" that resembled a loo. So, at a certain moment, people chose a room, usually a big room, and transformed it into a bathroom. This meant that there was plenty of space, so plenty of things ended up there.'

Nicoletta's talent is for decorating and arranging the furniture and objects in the house, many of which the Calamais have collected during their travels; all through

Right **Vanni's talent for making useful and decorative objects extends to the circular table in a sheltered garden spot beside a stone wall, which is lit in the evening by a cleverly contrived hanging metal lamp.**

Opposite **In a telling juxtaposition of new and old, a scooter – the quintessential symbol of modern Italy – is parked in a stone-walled barn that has stood for many hundreds of years.**

Below **Vineyards stretch away from the tower house for as far as the eye can see.**

the house are interesting objects, charmingly arranged with quirky combinations and juxtapositions of colour, texture and shape.

Nicoletta has a talent for arranging the space outside as well, dividing the area surrounding the tower into comfortable and relaxing areas from which to view the ever-changing landscape or simply to sit and relax. Many of these areas are furnished with tables made by Vanni, using the bases of local wine barrels.

La Torre del Chito is a genuinely relaxed and hospitable home. 'Although sometimes I think wistfully of a modern, well-equipped flat where everything works,' says Nicoletta, 'I soon remember how much we love our old house – the space, the views and its warmth, even in winter. We are very happy here.'

This page and opposite **A** *delicately painted fresco sweeps around all the walls of an upstairs bedroom. Thought to date from the 18th century, it depicts swallows, both in flight and at rest in a garden, appearing much as they do as they swoop around the house today. The restoration of the frescoes, hidden under many years of paint, was both painstaking and lengthy, involving many buckets of tepid water and much patience.*

a haunt of swallows

Carlo Musso is a 'green' architect, one who specializes in the detailed and careful restoration of old houses; his wife, Fulvia, is a teacher. The house they have restored in the Tuscan hamlet of Colle di Buggiano reflects today the disciplines of both their professions, having been brought back to life with both knowledge and patience.

Carlo and Fulvia had been looking in the area for over two years when they came on L'Antica Casa le Rondini – the House of the Swallows. It seemed perfect. As Carla says, 'It had never been restored before and everything was original. The village was like the house – it was entirely medieval, car-free and very peaceful. And of course swallows nested here, swooping and diving around the house.'

Opposite the house is an unusual joy in a medieval village – a walled garden with olive and cypress trees where families gather and sit. In classic Tuscan style, the village sits on a hilltop surrounded by olive

Frescoes on the walls of the main bedroom depict swallows both at rest and in flight, echoing the swooping birds outside.

groves, and Le Rondini, near the summit of the hill, looks down over the landscape beyond. There is not much to the place. Three streets – one of which passes beneath Le Rondini, through an archway – all lead to the square, which has a church, a restaurant and a bar.

Since the house had not been inhabited for 40 years, most of the original structure was intact, as was much else, including the kitchen fire, which was what Fulvia initially fell in love with. The couple set out to do the minimum work necessary to make Le Rondini suitable for modern living. Once they had started though, they found – as is so often the case – that there was much more to do than they had envisaged. 'As we worked, we uncovered the wonderful 300-year-old ceiling of cypress wood and tiles, as well as the stonework that

Far left Fulvia and Carlo Musso have been careful to decorate the house in a way sympathetic to its age and appearance. This bathroom is painted in soft pinks, complementing the early wall paintings of stylized leaves that frame the room in panels.

Left Much of the furniture for Le Rondini was already in Fulvia and Carlo's possession, and it all looks as though it has been in the house for many years. This wrought-iron bed, a light, flowing example of its type, is perfectly at home in a bedroom of lightly frescoed panels.

This page and opposite **Part of the overriding charm of Le Rondini for Fulvia Musso was the existence of part of the original kitchen, including the kitchen fire complete with old ovens and storage spaces. A heavy beam runs across the whole of the fireplace wall and is used by Fulvia as a display shelf for some of her collection of old pottery and ceramics.**

surrounds the door and window frames, which was covered by paint, and which we sandblasted away.' Carlo is known for his interest in combining traditional materials with ecologically friendly systems and was therefore keen to install solar panels to make best use of the power of the Tuscan sun, but it was not to be. 'Unfortunately the law that protects historical sites does not allow the exterior aspect of the house to be changed, so we decided to use natural gas instead.' They were able, however, to restore and repair the old garden cistern to catch and store rainwater.

One of the present pleasures of the house is the evocative kitchen that looks as though it has always been as it is now, although in fact much work has been done by Carlo and Fulvia. 'The kitchen was originally two rooms, but was enlarged by installing an archway to open up the dividing wall. The original fire and cooking stove remained and, being still in good working order, are used during the winter; at the opposite end of the room we have built a new kitchen, made from reclaimed materials, with a sink of Carrara marble, with smaller pieces of marble used to make up the work surfaces.'

The sitting room was also enlarged, by knocking down a non-original wall which had divided the space into two small rooms. As they did that work, they discovered, to their great pleasure, the original floor of 'beautifully worn' terracotta tiles, as well as some

stencilled frescoes. They found other frescoes too, the most important of which date back to the 18th century, covering the walls of the main bedroom, and depicting swallows in flight, echoing the swooping birds outside. To restore the frescoes, Fulvia painstakingly removed each layer of paint with tepid water over nine months – a long job but one in which the end result more than justified the means.

Since they planned to take paying guests, Carlo and Fulvia wanted the restoration of Le Rondini to be sensitive and sympathetic to its past, allowing the beauty of the original features to take centre stage. Colour choice was important in such an atmospheric house and Fulvia trod carefully, basing the scheme in one frescoed room on the colours of the original design; the colours of the other rooms were inspired by the predominant colours in the hand-painted tiles. They already had most pieces of furniture, which they augmented from local markets, and many of the curtains were embroidered by Fulvia's mother. The whole house is indeed, as Fulvia calls it, a work perfectly in keeping with its past.

Above left and opposite **During restoration, many of the doors were found to be framed with surrounds made of** pietra serena, *a type of stone much used locally. Carlo and Fulvia uncovered these surrounds and painted the adjacent walls in colours that blended with and complemented the doorways.*

Above and top **Colle di Buggiano and other nearby hamlets have many fine examples of medieval architecture; little seems to have changed over the centuries.**

stylish
simplicity

In some cultures, 'stylish simplicity' would be a contradiction in terms, but it makes sense to the Italians since they virtually invented the idea – and translated it into a look that is neither as brutal as minimalism nor as fussy as much traditional decoration. Stylish simplicity is a softer-edged, easier way of living, combining the new and innovative with much of the best of the rest, resulting in spare, clean interiors where modern design is used in a disciplined way.

A stylishly simple interior may consist of all that is new, but it may also have a mix of old favourites and new enthusiasms, edited into a purity of composition, sometimes combined with other styles and periods, sometimes standing alone. This approach has long prevailed in Italian cities, but today's rural interiors are as likely to be pared down and refined as their city cousins. The difference is that modern simplicity, country-style, is as much affected by what is outside as by what is in. Often, faced with the dramatic scenery and glaring contrasts of summer light and shade, country dwellers choose pale soothing tones of stone and cream, which also emphasize the more neutral tones used in furnishings. Stylish simplicity in the country is nothing if not practical, nothing if not pragmatic.

a light and airy loft

Architect Sebastian Abbado's house in Tuscany is the proverbial bolt-hole. Once a barn used for the storage of farm machinery, it has been converted by him into a serene, light-filled retreat – a place that he can use as a base for his creating his art and sculpture.

When Sebastian Abbado found his house, close to the home of his mother, Gabriella (see pages 170–77), it was a machinery store only in name; nothing remained except the perimeter and the foundations. But that was enough for him to work on. In common with many other areas of Europe, in this part of Italy new building is permitted only within the original foundations of an existing building, and in the style of the original – which was, in this case, not much style at all, 'It was built in the mid-20th century and not very interesting,' says Sebastian. Not that he found this daunting – his architectural background meant that he looked at the project with interest rather than alarm.

'This is to be my private Tuscan den and it is, up to a point, a work-in-progress. It was meant to be a simple enclosure although it didn't turn out quite like that. It isn't finished yet – it's one of those places that constantly develops, but it will eventually become exactly

Left At one side of the living area is an all-purpose Tuscan table flanked by a church bench whose proportions make the two a fine match. An old metal hatstand is hung with empty picture frames as well as hats.

Below The textured concrete floor is covered with natural woven rugs, and each object in the room has a practical as well as a decorative purpose. Above the doors are framed tapestries emphasizing the architectural qualities of the mix.

Above **Looking down from the gallery stairs into the ground-floor space, the precision of the placing of the furniture and objects can be appreciated. In the foreground is a distinctly Sebastian Abbado touch: a witty chandelier of red roses designed by Lorenzo Capaccio.**

Above right and opposite **Cleverly used to drape over beds and hang at the window, Sebastian's collection of textiles come into their own in the bedrooms. All the bedrooms have floors of resin-coated concrete that has had pigment rubbed into it, and which gives the appearance of rich, old, polished tiles. In this bedroom, off the living area, the bed was designed by Sebastian.**

what I want.' It has developed, and doubtless will continue to do so because, if you give a project of this nature – be it a restoration or even a reclamation – to an architect, he will view it in a very different light from how it would be seen by a painter or an interior decorator. An architect's training teaches him to make the best use of all available space – to find alternative uses for that which is already there and alternative solutions to any problems that might arise. Sebastian was very clear in his own mind about what he wanted: 'I didn't want a townhouse or a very modern, minimalist place; it was to be light, and at the same time I wanted to keep the space itself sparse and furnished with essentials – pieces that each had their own space and were important enough to stand alone.'

This he has done: the simple pieces of furniture are well positioned, looking as he hoped – a little theatrical and sculptural at the same time. He dislikes rooms that are too full: 'If it's an object or even a blank wall, if it has something to say (and even a wall can speak), or if it has a purpose or a reason – then it can have a place here.'

Cleverly, each piece seems completely at home: 'I don't like it when an interior looks too researched or too obvious. Old houses that are completely modernized with new furniture seem to have lost their way, as do houses decorated the other way around – modern buildings with old things carefully placed within them never

Opposite **Pride of place in this room is taken by the Italian iron bed dated from the early 19th century; green-painted Italian chairs stand at the feet.**

Above and above left **A range, antique in appearance but modern in design, dominates the kitchen area. The relatively sparse decorative effect in evidence throughout the house is deliberate. Sebastian wanted only pieces of furniture and accessories that could hold their own and were attractive in their own right.**

seem to work.' The house today is perhaps larger than he originally envisaged. It has two double bedrooms with their own bathrooms, a single bedroom and a bed in an upper gallery. Downstairs there is a large living area that incorporates a kitchen space, which is fitted with an ingenious stove, similar in type to an Aga – a replica range that both heats the area and can be used for cooking.

The materials, such as the textured-concrete floors, are equally carefully thought out. Sebastian seeks to use natural materials where he can and chooses colours with a purpose: 'I like to use new varnishes, unusual pigments and colour to get a contrived ancient/modern look – again something that is appropriate to the building and the setting. I want colours and textiles that come from the landscape around the house, the weather and the seasons. I think of the colours that I have used so far as a base for building up more colour. It's a bit like doing a painting really.'

The simple, serene space suits its purpose perfectly: to act as a retreat, perhaps, but also as a place where Sebastian's work as an artist can constantly be refined.

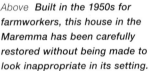 *Above Built in the 1950s for farmworkers, this house in the Maremma has been carefully restored without being made to look inappropriate in its setting.*

Right The master bedroom carries the owner's decorative signature: an inspirational mix of past and present. The past is shown in the lace cushions and the panelling; modern design is represented in a bedside light by Mark Brazier-Jones.

Opposite Glimpsed from the bedroom, the deep rounded bath, designed by Philippe Starck, stands on a floor of whitewashed oak boards. Above hangs a flamboyantly grand 19th-century French chandelier.

understated grace

The Italian countryside is as varied as it is beautiful. Although there are areas that epitomize the traditional landscape known to admirers of Renaissance painting, other parts are very different. The Maremma is just such a distinct region, where the land itself is low, swampy almost, as it rolls down towards the sea.

The owner of this house in the Maremma – for a long time unknown to many Tuscany-lovers – is an interior designer who co-manages Contemporanea, a gallery and shop in Rome. Contemporanea specializes in the distinctive and modern, including witty pieces by English designer Mark Brazier-Jones, known for his original ironwork creations.

Grounded in a small grove of olives, the house stands square and confident in the flat landscape, just outside the old hilltop town of Capalbio. It does not conform to the conventional idea of the Italian farmhouse. For one thing, it is not especially old –

Left **The kitchen's textured wall surface, created in the same way as that of the dining room, makes a good contrast with the sink, created from a block of basalt. The floor is of travertine slabs, cut against the grain, creating a rough surface.**

Above, above left and opposite **The dining room, part of a new extension added about five years ago, has walls created by adding colour to a water base and applying the mixture to wet plaster. The table's base is by British designer Mark Brazier-Jones.**

having been built in the 1950s – and, for another, it was not built for a farming family, but erected by the local council for farmworkers to live in while they were draining the swamps of the Maremma, after which time they were able to work the land. Each family was granted a house with 4,000 square metres (4,780 square yards) of land. From these somewhat unpromising foundations, the interior designer from Rome has shaped a country residence that combines simplicity and stylish design with a complete lack of pretension.

As far as the exterior was concerned, it was important to the owner and her family that the restored house should be in keeping with the spirit of the surrounding region. Although they added a small wing to accommodate living and dining areas, in other respects, she explains, 'We tried to leave the structure much as we found it, since the local architecture and profile is very low-key; we decorated the outside of the house in a way that, we hoped, would give the impression that it had simply evolved over the passage of time.'

Above **Simple canvas directors' chairs are an amusing and pleasing contrast to the heavy, bulbous-legged table.**

Right **In one corner of the living room, the soft hue of the French painted cabinet dating from the 18th century is emphasized by the pale travertine marble stairs that climb around it; the plaster fireplace in the foreground is a Contemporanea design.**

Opposite **At the other end of the room is a clutch of fine objects, including a plastered-wood cabinet with doors by Gennaro Avallone in plaster over canvas. On the cabinet, next to an empty frame by the Japanese designer Mineko, is a head cast by Oliviero Rinaldi. The white leather bench and cushions are from Contemporanea.**

In the interior, elements of the past were chosen to reflect the area's history, while elements of the present make themselves felt in the quirky juxtaposition of objects. The owner boldly decided to create a doorless enfilade between the downstairs rooms – a device that increases the sense of space while retaining the notion of simple living and working areas. The master bedroom is a success story in miniature: a tiny room with just enough space for a bed; a door facing the bed opens to reveal a vast bathtub in a tiny cupboard. It is a witty reversal of the usual arrangement.

The decoration is what the owner calls 'minimalist baroque'. It is almost monastic in feel, but with an air of relaxed comfort – all very much in the style of the owner's gallery in Rome. It is a triumphant attempt to challenge the conventional idea of 'country style' and to create an informal, modern version of a comfortable rural interior. In every room the colour palette is pale, veering towards the neutral, but with contrasts of texture and shade that soften the edges of what might otherwise be too hard-lined, with changes in floor surfaces and wall tones. Nothing has been done without a reason – from kitchen to bedrooms, every object, every detail, has been considered at length, every piece of furniture chosen with care.

This page **The flat plains of the Maremma are quite unlike the hilly landscape more usually associated with Tuscany. They have a soothing, peaceful aspect and project an air of calm and silence.**

Above and left **The main bedroom has a beamed ceiling and a loft area above a small ensuite bathroom. The tufa-coloured walls are emphasized by pale grey door surrounds.**

Right **Ilaria designed the living-room sofas and cleverly covered them with two jewel colours in linen from Ian Mankin. The wall colour was created by adding pigment to wet plaster.**

a haven of harmony

It takes a measure of confidence and enormous skill, as well as buckets of those imponderables, style and taste, to demolish a house and start again almost from architectural and decorative scratch. It is even harder to end up with a house that is both characterful and comfortable, as well as being extremely pretty. But Ilaria Miani has achieved all her aims.

Casellacce is an invention – a fact that Ilaria Miani, well-known interior designer and owner of a Rome-based furnishing company, is proud to acknowledge, for it is an invention with charm and elegance, of a type not often seen in an ordinary country house.

The house had originally been reconstructed in the 1930s. 'We decided to demolish it and rebuild it in more fitting style,' explains Ilaria. The interior is characterized by all-round elegance. Elegant may not seem the most appropriate word to describe a rustic Italian country house – but to be elegant is to be refined and defined, to be edited and disciplined, and all these qualities are found at Casellacce. It is also extremely contemporary in feel; although often used pejoratively, the adjective contemporary is used here with a sense of admiration.

'In rebuilding the house, we kept in mind some elements of the original architecture – the central staircase, for example, and the kitchen, which retains the original heavily beamed ceiling – but the rest was laid out within the existing framework,' says Ilaria. The kitchen was converted from what was formerly the stable building.

With the exception of a few family items, most of the pieces in the house are Ilaria's work, from the living-room sofas to some of the beds and the long bench in the entrance hall. She comments that the restoration of Casellacce has been what she calls an interesting synergy – 'not only using pieces from my existing range here, but also

being able to test out new ideas that I have then put into my ranges.'
Throughout the house, the plaster walls have been coloured with
pigment while the plaster was still wet – a traditional method of
adding colour to an interior, and a technique that is still as effective
and eye-catching today as it ever was.

Ilaria is good at colour – very good – and she has cleverly used
colour on the walls and in her choice of textiles, that work together
in counterpoint. She has done this by keeping the colour of the walls
muted and using fabric colour as accent: 'Every room has a special
view, and the landscape and light filling every window are the best

*Above**In this almost organic
scene in the entrance hall of
Casellacce, everything – from
the wall paint to the wooden
pegboard and bench, the
stacked baskets and the coats
– seems touched by the same
earthbound colour palette.*

pictures and the best light that you could have; for that reason I have kept the colour scheme for the walls and furniture very soft: grey for the ground floor and a sort of tufa [limestone] colour for the first floor.'

The fabrics that she chose for the house were an entirely different matter: 'It was in the textiles that I introduced strong colours: pink, orange, lilac, fuchsia and purple. I wanted them to cause surprise, give enjoyment, and add life and energy to daily living. A cupboard can look very serious from the outside, but here, when you open it, you will find something unexpected – there will be coloured, painted stripes, or it will be lined with a quilted fabric. A bed may be constructed to a simple design, but the sheets and covers should be sumptuous or colourful.'

In the restoration of Casellacce, Ilaria has been inspired by the work of the late American artist and sculptor Donald Judd, who espoused the philosophy of 'empty volume'. She has consequently sought to keep the interior architecturally clean and completely devoid of clutter, with every piece of furniture thoughtfully placed.

It has a powerful personality, this house, and it is comfortable with its simplicity; every element has been carefully chosen, from the furniture to the fabrics, and every element is plainly and simply harmonious.

Opposite **This is an 'infinity pool' that really lives up to its name; the view from this well-designed piece of water is one of a never-ending landscape.**

Below **Outside, a wooden table in the shade has been teamed with traditional French wooden slatted garden chairs; beyond, a rather surreal pergola shades some comfortable sun chairs.**

Left and inset **The same sense of order that pervades the public areas of La Scuola is evident in bedrooms of almost monastic austerity, were it not for the luxurious bedding and linen. The six bedrooms in La Scuola are havens of peace and silence. In this one, the beds are French, their swirling iron curves emphasized by the imaginative and unusual mirror, made from a mansard window.**

an old school story

Mimmi O'Connell's retreat in the Val d'Orcia is a former school in the village of San Casciano dei Bagni: 'I loved the space of La Scuola; I wanted it as soon as I saw it,' says the designer. 'I once had a farmhouse in the village but this is different.'

La Vecchia Scuola, as it is sometimes known in the village, translates as 'the former school' rather than 'the charmingly old school' – and, on the outside at least, it is not particularly charming at all. Built in the 1960s and designed, like many buildings of the period, for function rather than form, it is municipal in style, box-like and totally devoid of the nostalgic aura that permeates other, older country dwellings.

All that is fine with Mimmi O'Connell. She has already done the Tuscan farmhouse thing and moved on, and, as a modern designer of verve and invention, the open spaces and spatial qualities of the building – in particular, its long corridor, in which you can still sense the sound of small, clattering feet – acted like

Left **The colours that make up the original terrazzo floor in the corridor inspired the colour scheme that Mimmi chose for the rest of the house.**

Below **Contrasting styles and periods are evident in the area for winter dining. While the chairs came from an English public school, the new table, with its zinc top, is by Conran, and the exotic candlesticks are from 16th-century Mongolia.**

Opposite **Both of these beds were designed by Mimmi and made in Tuscany. The painting, The Visitor, is by Sally Green.**

a magnet on her acquisitive and decorative senses: 'The chance to make a house out of 560 square metres (6,000 square feet) of space, all on one floor, was one I couldn't miss – and a house with double-height ceilings, and fabulous views into the bargain.'

So Mimmi bought the school and set about getting the measure of the place. She wanted to make it into a comfortable house, while retaining the idea that it had been a working building.

The school's architecture informed the design and decoration, which Mimmi felt should be disciplined and simple. So she cut new openings into the walls where previously there had been none, she replaced school windows with French windows, and she built a fireplace inside. For the summer living area she created a portico and a pool area, reached from the house through four French windows

and lined with local travertine, with woodwork painted grey; meals are taken here on large tables designed by Mimmi and made from scaffolding planks.

'I wanted to continue the sense of discipline that still hung in the air,' she says. The school corridor was a constant reminder of the building's original function, and Mimmi wanted it to dictate, or at least to influence, the design and decoration. The floor of the corridor was the original, indestructible terrazzo – disliked by some for its industrial connotations, but liked by the designer for its association with the building's former life.

Mimmi has allowed the colour in the terrazzo to dictate the internal colour scheme – a combination of greys, terracotta, beige and a chalky white. Elsewhere, in each of the bedrooms (all former classrooms leading off the main

Top **Always a stickler for detail, Mimmi has had special plates designed and made particularly to be used in La Scuola.**

Above **The school corridor with its original floor has deliberately been left unadorned except for the Indonesian door at the end, flanked by locally made lanterns.**

Right **The living area, furnished with distinctive 19th-century scholarback chairs, is part of what was formerly the teachers' common room. Mimmi has kept the original terrazzo floor, which is warmed by a new fireplace that she designed and installed.**

corridor), she has used matt white on the walls, with glossy white on the deep skirting boards. She never hangs paintings; they are always left propped up against the walls.

Mimmi is known for her love of simple, clean graphic design and simple decorative ideas, so in many respects the disciplined and strongly functional lines of a modern school space make a wonderful background for all her decorative ideas. It is also a perfect background for her collection of Indonesian art – such as the oversized pair of 18th-century horses and their riders, the antique, wooden wild boars, the old baskets and water containers. At the end of the otherwise unadorned corridor hangs an ornate and ornamental door from Lombok – a dramatic touch.

The severity of the design is touched throughout by softer details such as linen sheets and luxurious white towels, 19th-century Welsh blankets and bold Welsh quilts with intricate patterns – all of which come from her own shop, Port of Call in London. And there is comfort in the technology, too. A wall in one room is unapologetically dominated by a large plasma television.

Left and above **The building's former scholastic incarnation had meant that not much attention had been paid to the area surrounding the house. As well as a swimming pool, Mimmi wanted a shaded loggia along one side, so she designed a space that incorporated both shelter and a paved area around the pool, but laid it out in a way that did not detract from the striking woodland landscape that flanks the building.**

classic
elegance

To an Italian, elegance is an essential part of life; it is no surprise that the phrase *bella figura* is both immediately understandable and almost untranslatable – there being no equivalent in English or French. Elegance is not to do with a particular fashion; rather, it is a knowledge and a sense of what looks good that goes far beyond transient enthusiasms. Elegance is always simple; it is always less, never more – and it is always desirable.

Although elegance is international, it takes many different forms. The elegance of a Provençal country interior is not the same as that of a Parisian *maison particulier*, in the same way that the elegance of a New York apartment is not the elegance of a Cape Cod summer house. Equally, elegant Tuscan rural interiors are not the same as those of the cities of Tuscany; there is a softer approach, albeit touched with a certain urbanity. There is also an understanding of a local or native style, for elegance is always a question of using the best available – taking a pivotal piece and refining it, giving it a certain distinction, perhaps by placing it in a certain spot, in the right light, and surrounding it by objects that both complement and flatter it. It is not easy to describe, this elegance of touch, but, as in the following pages, when you see it – you know it.

a serene sanctuary

When the de Loozes first saw the early 19th-century building north of Siena, it was like many other Tuscan farmhouses that had been long abandoned, except that it was a good deal larger than most others of its kind, even boasting its own small chapel.

Some 20 km (12 miles) from the ancient walled city of Siena can be found Le Porciglia, a long, low, stone farmhouse typical of the area – but such a basic description does not at all convey the distinctive personality of the house, or explain why it made such a strong initial impression on interior decorator Simone de Looze and her husband, its current owners. The couple bought it on a whim, concluding within 24 hours of the first viewing that it was the house for them.

Having made their decision to buy Le Porciglia, the de Loozes contacted the English designer Anthony Collett of Collett–Zarzycki to help them make sense of the space architecturally. Noted for his cool, clean approach to architectural and interior design, Collett has a house of his own in Tuscany that reflects his design principles. With the added help of an Italian architect, the trilingual Carlos Rex – the

Above left **The farmhouse and garden were rebuilt from a former working farm, which once had a full complement of stables, barns and pigsties.**

Above and right **The large living room, decorated in pale neutral tones, is dominated by a fine 18th-century fireplace faced by two high-backed Dutch chairs from the same period. The pair of sofas are covered in unobtrusive white linen, allowing the many decorative pieces to take centre stage.**

Above **Along one wall of the living room is a table covered in Indian fabric. In the centre is a model of the Archangel Gabriel next to a Cretan dish and a heap of old French boules; on either side, two tall candlesticks have been turned into lamps, and an African carved wooden dog stands alone. The display also includes an item of 19th-century fencing armour.**

Top and top right **Hanging from the beams beyond the gallery, a 19th-century French chandelier from a hotel in the south of France swings in front of one of the bedrooms.**

Opposite **The elegant gallery is fitted with balustrading that once formed the balcony of an Italian theatre, which burnt down in the 1920s.**

only one who was capable of organizing and delivering the many permits that were needed – they worked out a scheme that would make the most satisfactory use of what was, in Simone's words, the 'rather ungainly' 1,000 square metres (10,800 square feet) of space. (In addition to the chapel, there were stables, pigsties and barns.) The de Loozes wanted to create a house that was comfortable and friendly but with enough room and space for everyone to enjoy.

The eventual design featured a house with four bedrooms and an adjoining guest cottage in what had originally been the hay barn. There would have been more than four bedrooms, had not one of the de Loozes' more unusual ideas been to create an airy, light, double-height living room in the main house, a room that soars up to the old beams; it includes a 19th-century chandelier that came from a hotel in the south of France. Facing onto this space are the remaining bedrooms, one with an iron balcony overlooking the central space, the others leading out onto a balustraded gallery, salvaged from a 20th-century Italian theatre that burnt down. It is dramatic – and certainly not what you might expect to find within the walls of a Tuscan farmhouse.

The restoration was not carried out at any great speed. In fact, Simone says, it took five years. But five years provides plenty of time to get things right, to reflect and sometimes to

Right **In one of the striking bathrooms, the marble bathtub, looking like something found in an ancient Roman villa, was in fact made in Livorno in the mid-18th century. The ornate tin mirror also comes from Livorno, but dates from a century later.**

Above **Built in along the length of the bath is a pair of alcoves for storing soap and potions; they are finished in early 20th-century tiles, hand-made and hand-painted in Sicily.**

Far right, above **Simone covered the tall bedheads of these old iron beds with red fabric and added narrow canopies to create dramatic frames.**

Far right, below **A large but unadorned bed has no bedhead; instead, Simone has hung behind it an Indian textile consisting of a motif of cypress trees set against a white background – a copy of the Punjabi original in the Victoria and Albert Museum in London. The bedcover is also white, with a naive rendition of fruit and flowers.**

It is a lovely house – calm and generous, grand in its concept of space, but comfortable in its use of it.

rethink – and the result will almost always be better than a job done in haste. In addition to being an experienced interior decorator, Simone is an antiques dealer, as was her mother before her, and her passion for traditional rural and country style goes back a very long way, so she was definite about what she wanted. 'While I was still a little girl, I started to collect clippings from interiors magazines, and over all the years my taste for the things I'd like in a southern European country house has not changed.'

Simone wanted to use a neutral palette. 'I'm not particularly keen on the use of a great deal of colour in rustic-style houses; the objects and furniture all have their own story to tell, and they do that better against a neutral background.'

The neutral background was intended to set off many pieces of rustic antique furniture – Italian yes, but also Dutch and French. 'Just like my mother, I've

Above **Simone collects country furniture from all over Europe. On the top of a 17th-century cupboard from the Italian region of Le Marche, which retains its original colour, are pots from Puglia. To make the floor, Simone used new terracotta tiles turned upside down and set in beige cement.**

Right **The lovely vaulted ceiling of the kitchen gives it a grace and lightness not often seen in such buildings; the arches separate the cooking area from the dining space, which is simply furnished with a long table made by Piet Hein Eek and chairs from Indonesia.**

Far right **There are two sinks in the kitchen area. The smaller is surrounded by hand-made Sicilian tiles; the larger is made to measure from stone.**

developed a liking for country furniture that literally falls apart.' If that is the case, the various fragile pieces must have been repaired with great efficiency; there is little evidence in the elegantly furnished rooms of make-do-and-mend.

Perhaps this reflects Simone's other skill – the arrangement of rooms, the most important attribute of an accomplished interior decorator. As Simone says, 'As an antiques dealer, one learns that decorating is all about the right objects put together in the right way. Even a "wrong" room can be made "right" if it has fantastic stuff in it.'

Apart from the confident design of the interior space, there are numerous other architectural elements that catch the eye, such as the floors, particularly a floor that looks like a wide-spaced chequerboard of old terracotta tiles. Simone designed this with new tiles that have simply been turned upside down and set into cement that has been tinted beige. 'It was a dream to

Above and opposite **Terraces and gardens have been made entirely from scratch – not something that is immediately apparent. Having originally been a large working farm, Le Porciglia is blessed with a number of outbuildings, from barns to piggeries, the elements of which – old stone walls, gently rounded arches, and so on – lend an added architectural interest to the sheltered outdoor eating and seating areas.**

experiment with the floors in Le Porciglia. On this floor we put old or new cotto tiles into coloured cement, but the variations are endless.' In keeping with the cool feel of the house, textiles are not a dominant feature of the design, but eye-catching pieces crop up everywhere, many of which have been collected by Simone from all over the world.

It is a lovely house – calm and generous, grand in its concept of space, but comfortable in its use of it. It is Simone's version of Italian country style, which involves a rethinking of the function and form of a contemporary country house, brought about by the introduction of an individual, personal style which seamlessly manages to relate the present to the past in a sophisticated, simple manner, and even more cleverly manages to the avoid the usual country house clichés. There are certain things that she insists upon: 'No chintz curtains, no hunting prints, and never, never, modern bathrooms.'

Right **On a plain terracotta floor, above an antique piano, is an oversized, highly decorative plaster relief, balanced by a collection of unrelated pieces on the piano. The composition is completed by the curved lines of an unusual horned chair.**

a feast of textures

Above **Montalcino today looks and feels almost organic, as if it has just risen, ready formed, from the Tuscan hillside.**

Opposite **The living room is furnished and decorated with Piero's typical confidence; one colour palette only has been used, based on the ochre of the walls; the interest lies in floor and furniture textures and the variety of designs and patterns used in a single scheme.**

Montalcino is a beautiful house restored by the renowned Italian architect and decorator Piero Castellini Baldissera. Attracted by a setting that includes 'a 360-degree view across the best of the Tuscan landscape', he has succeeded in bringing that view, and the textures and colours of the landscape, into the house itself.

Like Lavacchio (see pages 132–39), another property restored by Piero Castellini, Montalcino was once an abandoned farmhouse. Built in the 18th century to shelter livestock, it was not a particularly imposing building, set in the middle of agricultural land in the centre of the Tuscan countryside. It did however benefit from its position overlooking the famous rolling hills that are punctuated, just as they were 400 years ago, with dark cypress trees and old, semi-ruined stone buildings.

It was evident that major restoration was needed. Happily for the house, Piero Castellini Baldissera is a determined and focused architect with a very clear idea of what he wanted to achieve – which was, above all, a house that, while reflecting its

Above and right **The small dining room provides a cool haven in summer when the heat is too fierce, and acts as a comfortable retreat at other, chillier times of the year.**

Far right **On an upstairs landing, an Empire daybed, covered in a contemporary striped fabric, has been placed beneath a set of 18th-century black and white prints of pastoral scenes.**

good age and provenance, would also be comfortable, light-filled and attractive. Although much of the house was in ruins, it was possible to retain the original floors and ceilings, as well as most of the walls. Great care was taken to augment remnants with the best possible local materials that would enhance and even ameliorate the original.

Today Montalcino is a commanding country house, with a vaulted-ceiling living room that runs across most of the ground floor, and with windows and doors that open on three sides to the grounds beyond. Also on the ground floor are a small, pretty dining room and a cool, practical kitchen. Upstairs is a series of bedrooms, each with its own bathroom. Although each is decorated in a different colour scheme, they share a wonderful coolness – with tiled floors, muted tones on the walls and unlined curtains on the beds and at the windows, which let the air circulate throughout the rooms.

Outside, running along the length of one side of the house, is a shaded dining loggia and a terrace for sitting and reading as well as eating, drinking and entertaining.

The furniture is a mix of new and comfortable, old and beautiful, and downright quirky. It is unified with upholstery and soft furnishings chosen to work together within particular soft colour palettes.

Colour is a skill at which Piero excels. His inspiration comes from what he sees around him: the ochre tones of the sun and the red and terracotta pinks of the earth and stones. Elsewhere, on his travels, Piero is inspired by the strong colours of the Mediterranean lands as well as the vibrant, immediate colours of the Orient; all these he has taken, mixed together, softened and applied to the walls, creating a varied effect that effortlessly changes from room to room.

He works the same magic with textiles, relying sometimes on traditional classical patterns, such as 18th-century stripes or toiles, but also creating his own designs in the same palette and tradition that are designed to work in this kind of house.

Apart from his architectural and decorative skills, Piero delights in collecting the strange, the quirky and the individual, and combining them – old and new, valuable and not so valuable. This process gives

Above **One of the beds, which features faux bamboo posts, is simply hung with muslin; there is no other decoration in the room except for a chair covered in a dramatic toile de Jouy print.**

Right **Piero's eclectic decorative style is well demonstrated here on a small landing, where he has placed a 20th-century chair with horn legs and arms directly beneath an example of the real thing – stuffed, of course.**

Opposite **The simplicity of the painted blue and white stripes on the walls of this bedroom, combined with natural white bed hangings and plain linen curtains, means that the bed itself can carry a much bolder blue and white toile de Jouy quilted cover, as well as a pair of exuberant printed cotton cushions in the same style.**

him pleasure, the shapes and materials sometimes grouped by a unifying colour, sometimes by a theme, and sometimes juxtaposed to provide an original or amusing contrast. Pictures are hung for effect – in one room, a group of botanical prints are tightly massed; in another, 18th-century portraits in grisaille are hung against the strongest of ochre walls. It sums up the house – wherever you look, there is something to amuse or admire.

Overall the story of the house is a story of texture – both in the contrasts and in the relationships between elements. In every single room, the floors, walls, textiles and colours work together; the furniture and furnishings, the pictures and objects all complement each other with ease. Outside, too, the architectural elements contrast with the textures of the natural elements – the plants, the vines, the trees.

Left At the kitchen end of the house, on a rough-tiled floor, is a practical all-weather hat stand, with foot and head gear appropriate for any weather, summer and winter.

Below The proliferation of outbuildings and barns means that Montalcino is blessed with a three-sided courtyard that provides a sheltered area at the back of the house.

Right One side of the house is sheltered by the old three-sided courtyard; here, climbing plants from roses to vines grow in profusion across the walls and around the doors.

the height of rural chic

'I wasn't exactly given a brief,' says Paola Navone. 'It was rather that a friend who works in the Milan fashion industry said that he had a wonderful opportunity to move to the country, and asked me to help him with the house. I knew his life well, so I could envisage what he might want in a rural setting. It was left totally up to me. I could make of it what I wanted.'

Above and right **The living room, with its pale honey walls and traditional beamed and tiled ceiling, is dominated by two French clock faces from an old church tower, found by Paola in a Paris flea market. The modern sofas are covered in rough linen from her collection of textiles, specially dyed to a soothing shade of grey-green.**

Above **The entrance to the library – which was once, in a former life, the piggery – is dominated by two huge, almost ghostly paintings of figures. The tones of the paintings are complemented by the soft greys used on the skirting boards and also on the once-dark beams.**

Right **Another exercise in clever use of tonal colours is this brick vaulted space, with soft apricot walls, now used as a dining room. An interesting contrast in textures combines metal table and chairs with a tiled floor. The room is lit by an extravagantly decorative chandelier.**

Paola Navone is an architect and designer of renown, based in Milan and with commissions ranging from shops and offices to furniture and objects. She undertakes interiors only as part of a wider portfolio, but when a friend told her he had found a house near Montepulciano that he was determined to buy – and that he wanted her to turn into an interesting, and livable, country house for him, she took up the challenge. The owner was a successful Milanese businessman who, in Paola's words, 'works hard and travels hard'. The raw material was

Left **The master bedroom – this time painted in soft lilacs and blues – is dominated by a painted and gilded drapery in carved baroque style, found by Paola Navone in London. Its weight, both literally and decoratively, means that little else is needed in the room.**

Below **Different colour palettes evoke various moods. Some, as in the bedrooms and bathrooms, are peaceful and calming. The wisteria-toned bathroom is simplicity itself, with freestanding bath, metal tables for towels and bottles, and a metal towel rail, hung high on the wall.**

a former fortified farmhouse, complete with arrow slits and rifle holes, as well as a ground floor built to house sheep and pigs. Paola knew she would not be able to renovate in traditional style. 'My first concern was how the house should look as a whole. Tuscan style is thought of as having a certain severity – it is a beautiful area but the houses are associated with dark wood and dark rooms. So I wanted to countermand that and to

create an environment that was the opposite of severe – somewhere calm and relaxed, a place where this man could happily live, and have his own things around him.'

She decided that colour was the tool as well as the answer. Her chosen palette seems almost to have more in common with the warm colours of Provence than the earthy colours so often seen in Tuscany. 'I decided to use colour not only to lift

Above **Behind a simple divan bed, a broad horizontal stripe has been painted instead of a conventional bedhead.**

Right **Even a simple passage and doorway become part of the colour-themed whole, painted as they are in shades that accentuate the simplicity of the setting.**

The fabrics convey an air of rural but sophisticated informality – dyed, rough linen on living-room sofas and, in bedrooms, chairs loose-covered in striped cotton sheeting found in Corfu.

Right **A sitting area next to a guest bedroom on the upper floor has a ceiling painted in a milky solution that gives the beams an almost bleached appearance. Visible in the far wall of the bedroom is a rifle hole dating from the time when this was a fortified farmhouse; it now has a Perspex cover to keep out draughts.**

the spirits but also to define the different parts of the house. I gave each group of rooms its own set of colours. There is a studio area, where the colours go from mint green to citrus tones; while in the entrance and boot room I used a dark brick tone contrasted with a strong cobalt blue.'

Paola set out to make the whole house like a stage set, a place where the owner could not only keep his already large collection of art and antiques, but also where he could introduce new things found on his travels, and they would not look out of place. Thus, the living room is dominated by two oversized clock faces from a French church tower and the main bedroom boasts a large piece of baroque sculpture found in London. Paola sums up the restored house in a few words: 'It looks very simple but there is a sophistication.' Indeed there is, and what could be a more appropriate setting for a modern-day gentleman of Milan?

sweet repose

When, in the late 1980s, interior designer Ilaria Miani and her husband found the house known as Buon Riposo, it was nothing like it appears here. In fact, it was more or less a ruin – one of the many ruins that could then be found in this part of rural Italy.

Above **To link a reading area with the sitting room beyond, Ilaria designed a passage lined with bookshelves on both sides and around the entrance.**

Left **New ceiling beams were built to replace the originals in the main living room. Since the original ceiling was quite low, the height was increased by sinking the living-room floor.**

The Via Francigena was the great medieval road leading from France to Rome, and the Orcia valley was dotted with more than 20 resting places for pilgrims on their journey to the Holy City. As Ilaria and her husband, Giorgio, began to explore the ruin they had bought, they found evidence that Buon Riposo had once been something more than a peasants' dwelling – that on this site had once stood one of the pilgrims' houses of rest.

As the Mianis worked on the house, the strata of centuries of life began to emerge, yielding clues to the building's age and use, clues like the floor tiles found in one part of the house that were inscribed 'Fabio Carli, 1560' – the name of a local brick furnace of the period. Eventually they deduced that Buon Riposo had indeed been a dwelling in the 16th century, and had been added to in the 18th century, and partially restored in the early 20th century. It became clear that, were they to restore it anew, they needed to take its past into account and reflect in its restoration the different periods of its long life. 'As it was so

Above **The storage alcove in the bathroom is outlined with a broad band of white paint, making a subtle contrast with the cream-painted plaster wall.**

Above right **White-painted wooden pegs are fixed under a shelf; they are used to hang towels and bathroom pieces.**

Opposite **Seen through a door to the bathroom, against the same cream plaster wall, and on a terracotta tiled floor, a rather heavy antique wooden bed has been simplified by Ilaria and washed white. Like other decorative elements, the colours throughout Buon Riposo have been kept very simple.**

clearly an ancient house,' says Ilaria, 'we sought to return it to what must have been its perfect simplicity.' With this end in mind, they researched all the antiques dealers within a range of 150 kilometres (90 miles), visiting them in a quest for the most authentic materials – 'searching always for the right tiles, the right bricks, the right beams'.

Good fortune played its part in the restoration. At nearby Villa La Foce, owned by the Marchesa Iris Origo, there was a fresco depicting Buon Riposo in the 19th century, showing enough contemporary detail to give the Mianis a start, and the confidence that their restorative instincts were correct. From this, the reader will deduce that Ilaria and Giorgio were determined to return Buon Riposo to its former glory, or at any rate to restore it to a house that reflected its ancient and fascinating history. This meant that every aspect, every element, of the house had to be carefully considered.

Although Ilaria has chosen a neutral palette in most rooms, leaving the unique architectural features of the house to make their own mark, she has subtly added some colour through judicious use of textiles.

Take the problem of what furniture to use. Furniture is always something to be thought about with care in a restoration project of this kind and the mix of furniture here is unusual. One might have thought, for example, that, having uncovered the fascinating history of the house, the Mianis would have wished to look for very early pieces. But Ilaria had inherited pieces of 19th- and 20th-century furniture that she wanted to use; she is also a designer of furniture (see pages 72–81) and was anxious to design specific pieces for Buon Riposo

'What I wanted to avoid,' says Ilaria, 'was falling into the trap of creating fake rustic decoration — trying to reinvent a peasant style that, in Tuscany at any rate, never existed.'

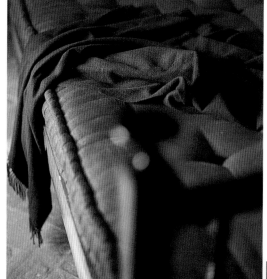

that were in keeping with the house's style and mood, and went with what else was there. 'I inherited some pieces from my grandmother and more from a family house in Cortina d'Ampezzo. My grandmother collected 19th-century furniture, and the Cortina house had been built in the 1940s by Tullio Rossi, a renowned architect of the day who designed all the furniture for the house as well, so that was that.

'But Buon Riposo is large and still more furniture was needed, so I began to design beds, tables and chairs to fill the gaps. I made the furniture to be both functional and flexible – often a modular piece that I could use in different ways in the same room, or move from one room to another. I like to change my houses to fit the mood of

Left **A clever decorative scheme involves five different fabric designs – all used in close proximity to each other and yet with no sense of excess; the secret is that they are all in the same colour combination of red and white, and four of them are based on geometric patterns.**

Right and above **In another example of Ilaria's adventurous use of colour, a deep-buttoned crimson mattress brightens up a dark wooden daybed.**

This page **Once a staging post for weary pilgrims, Buon Riposo has again become a place where guests can stop and relax under shade-giving trees, relishing the peace of the timeless landscape.**

the moment, and I enjoy experimenting. But the result of mixing furniture from all these different periods really is a pastiche!' A pastiche it may be, but it is far from contrived.

Colour is another of Ilaria's strengths. Although she has opted for a neutral palette in most rooms, leaving the unique architectural features of the house to make their own mark, she has subtly added some colour, particularly in the bedrooms, through judicious use of textiles. One bed has been draped with diaphanous copper-pink stripes, while the same colours are used in soft checks and floral patterns to cover chairs and stools, and another has a traditional buttoned mattress covered in a vibrant crimson and displayed to the world. As in the rest of the house, the finished effect is comfortable and subtle, creating a pleasing effect of timelessness.

This page and opposite **The original role of Buon Riposo as a staging post for coaches taking pilgrims to Rome is evident in its series of linked courtyards. Ilaria and Giorgio Miani were careful to respect the different architectural ages of Buon Riposo and to restore it with love and sensitivity.**

Above **Once an abandoned farmhouse, Lavacchio has lost none of its rural simplicity.**

Left **The long, low sitting room is dominated by a commanding stone fireplace surmounted by an evocative landscape.**

Far left **The striped fabric used on the daybed echoes the broad painted stripes on the wall; the vertical lines contrast with the subtle tiled floor.**

a gentleman's retreat

A successful blend of the traditional and the new is always hard to achieve, but for Piero Castellini Baldissera the genre holds no fears. An expert in the art of interior decoration, he is adept at mixing scale and shape, colour and texture into a harmonious whole, and one that is always in perfect taste.

Piero Castellini Baldissera is one of the masters of Tuscan restoration (see also pages 104–11, which describe his renovation of Montalcino). Whether it is because of his understanding of the landscape and the place that each house holds in it, or whether it is because of his love of traditional materials and colours, the houses that he brings back to life are always places of pleasurable calm and relaxation.

Lavacchio is a long, low farmhouse surrounded by a verdant orchard in amazingly beautiful countryside. From the outside, the house is unassuming, but once you are inside all is surprising. It was not always as comfortable as it is today, having been originally a home for cows; and, when Piero first saw it, it was abandoned and uninhabitable, even by cows. How things change! In his restoration of the building, Piero has cleverly kept all the best things about the house – its soul, the walls and floors, beams and windows, and worked around them, adding all the elements necessary for modern comfort.

Inside, textures and materials are of paramount importance. The central rooms have heavily beamed ceilings and the tiled floors have been restored and sealed. Throughout the house, furniture has been chosen with care and the details – always an area in which Piero excels – complement the furnishings with aplomb.

In the long living room with its low, beamed ceiling, the focal point is a fireplace – not a huge chimney piece in which food was once prepared, but an urban sophisticated piece that stands in contrast to the rustic surroundings. The chairs also are loose-covered and comfortable – library chairs, chairs that are used for reading and relaxing. This is the secret of Piero's style, the ability to create a sophisticated interior that is completely in keeping with the house's position and architectural heritage. Colour and its use are Piero's other most powerful tools – whether they are warm, earthy tones or cool, refreshing shades, he applies them

The secret of Piero's style is his ability to create a sophisticated interior that is completely in keeping with the house's position and architectural heritage.

with confidence. Sometimes a colour is textured, looking like the plaster itself, and sometimes it is applied in a pattern – more often than not, in a broad stripe, one of his decorative signatures and used on both walls and furniture.

The trick here is both the width of the stripe and the fact that it is always handpainted, which gives it depth and a delightful unevenness, in keeping with the relaxed surroundings. Stripes are sometimes in strong contrast and sometimes in complementary shades of a single

Left **Simplicity is one of Piero's watchwords, and there is never too much of anything. Here, the bath is fixed in the centre of the room flanked by a double curtain; although there are few modern gadgets, a comfortable chair and a practical towel rail are placed within easy reach.**

Above **An ornate traditional bed has curtains only, rather than being encumbered by a canopy, which would have hidden the curved iron arches. No rug is necessary. There are simply two tall reading lights and, at the foot of the bed, a comfortable stool.**

colour; they are always effective. This theme is continued in the fabrics; curtains and furnishings are all subject to stripes of different colours and depths – a timeless decorating secret.

Piero's other most distinctive skill lies in his attention to decorative detail. He is not interested in being purist, preferring to adopt a catholic approach to what should be considered decorative and what should not. He takes enormous pleasure in the arrangement of pictures, objects and decorative pieces, using them to create tableaux and conversation pieces on surfaces and walls, sometimes exhibiting a single object in solitary splendour or grouping like with like, using two, three or four of a kind together, and often using carefully chosen decorative cushions to pull the different groups together. The result is a house that is both comfortable and interesting – a true gentleman's country retreat.

Left *A full-length corner cupboard has been painted and decorated in semi-architectural style; the colour works perfectly with the ochre wall as well as with the grey-painted wooden daybed upholstered in complementary fabrics.*

Above left *In this small bedroom, broad hand-painted stripes on the walls are echoed by a simple curtain that does not overwhelm its surroundings.*

Right *An antique metal daybed has been transformed into a comfortable sofa with a thick, buttoned cushion in a striped fabric, bolsters and small cushions to match. A pair of bright, strongly patterned toile cushions establishes a link with the ochre walls.*

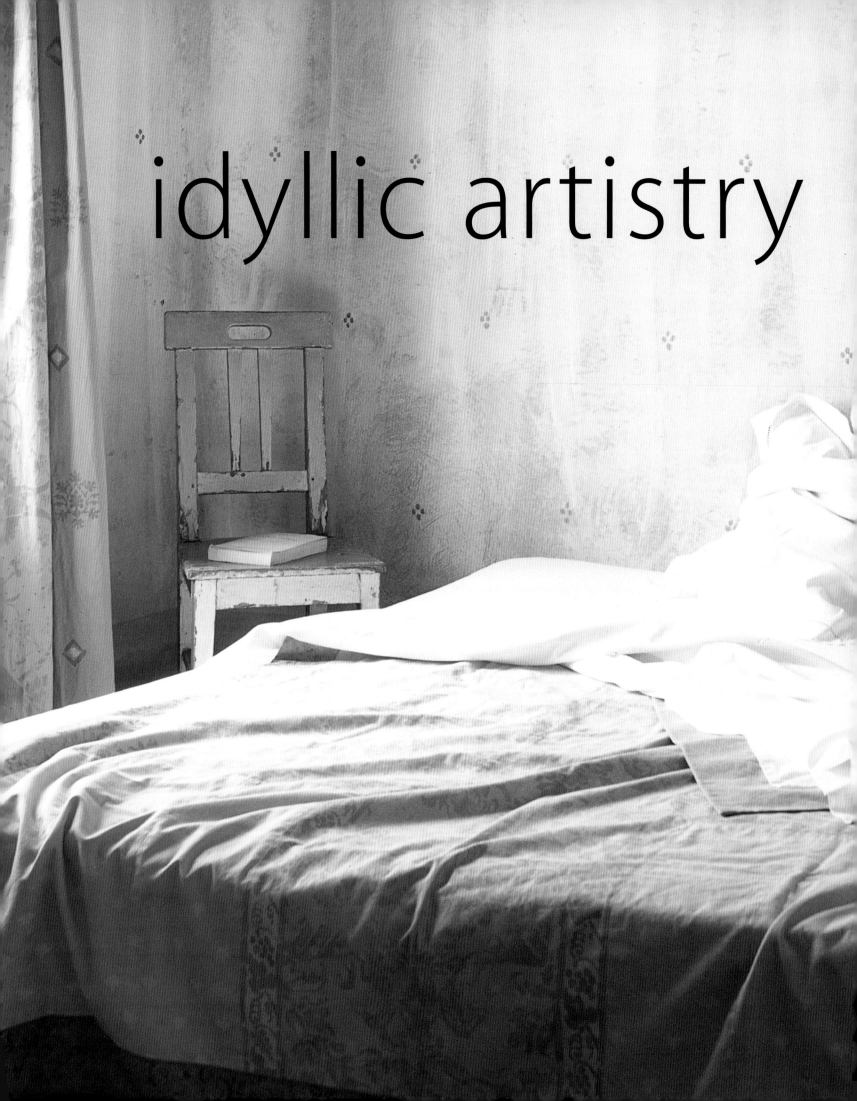

idyllic artistry

Italians have always been as interested in the applied arts as in the fine arts; for them, the beauty of a woven or printed textile, a decorated piece of glass or a table of unusual veneer is something to be celebrated and displayed as much as a painting or sculpture; and, when it comes to interior decoration, they like to use these beautiful and unusual pieces around them.

The owners of these artistic interiors, although seemingly different, have traits in common. They have all travelled widely; they have collected things wherever they have been; and they love to have around them the fruits of their experience. In their houses, all the elements — heirlooms, travellers' trophies and odd finds — have been put together with flair. The likely has been matched with the less likely, the grand with the humble, the old with the new; although the method might look haphazard, it needs considerable discipline. Putting things together well is often a matter of subtracting rather than adding, and of looking closely at each item to see what is unnecessary. It also needs confidence, both in one's own taste and in the intrinsic value of the objects to be arranged — a characteristic that all these owners possess.

beyond the rainbow

Walking into Marina Ferrara Pignatelli's Tuscan farmhouse is like walking through a rainbow into whatever may lie beyond; every room glows with clear colours, infused with light, cloaking the walls with tones that imperceptibly blend with those next to them. But the house was not always like this. Marina changed it into a home that is comfortable and welcoming as well as natural and uncontrived.

Marina discovered the house seven years ago. Her family roots lie in Tuscany and she had been keen to find a house in the region. 'I had been searching in Val D'Orcia and the surrounding area for more than two years, helped by some good friends who had already identified this incredible spot years before.'

The 'incredible spot' is a wild, unspoiled part of Tuscany, in the province of Siena, and Marina's house is backed by oak woods that extend right up to the edge of the property. In front of the house, the wide-open landscape, reminiscent of a 15th-century Sienese painting, stretches to encompass Mount Amiata and the Rocca di Radicofani. As Marina says, 'As far as the eye can go, there is no evidence of the 20th or 21st centuries to be seen.'

The farmhouse dates from the 17th century and, unusually, the structure had already been restored by an English owner when Marina took possession of it.

Above **There are views over a great swathe of countryside that appears almost uninhabited.**

Left **Marina has kept the garden scheme simple, adding more roses to those already there and planting regional species such as lavender and rosemary.**

Right **Marina has cushioned the raised stone surround in front of one of the original fireplaces, making an extra, comfortable space for lounging.**

Marina's role, as she saw it, was to do the interior decoration, landscape the garden and make a swimming pool. It was important to her that the house should be cosy and comfortable – Tuscany can be cold during the winter – and she therefore decided to keep the oldest part of the house, on the upper floor, as much as possible as it was when the farmers were still in residence. As luck would have it, the original brick floors were still there, as were the doors, beams and an open fireplace. This part of the house has now been arranged to accommodate three large bedrooms, three bathrooms, a living room and a small kitchen.

Above **A 19th-century baker's credenza or sideboard divides the kitchen part of the room from the dining area. The walls have been coloured by Marina in the traditional way, with hand-mixed paints; the rose colour on the upper walls contrasts with a deep green band painted up to dado level.**

The carpets were bought in exotic places such as Tibet, Syria and Turkey after hours of bargaining over tea and shish kebab. Most of the textiles came from India.

Right **The design of the kitchen focuses on simple concepts executed in a sophisticated way. Open shelves and wooden cupboards are used for storage, and the travertine sink is a contemporary interpretation of the traditional stone sink.**

Above **Since it was important to maintain the warmth and comfort of the kitchen in winter, the fireplace, with its pots and pans and other implements, was central to the whole room.**

Above **In the largest living room, formerly the main stables, an old credenza from Naples and a Syrian mirror are placed against an ochre-coloured wall. In lieu of a wooden door frame, a painted border runs around the door and around the base at skirting level.**

Above right and opposite **The seating in this room consists of large, low wooden bases with firm canvas seat cushions, on top of which are piles of assorted cushions covered in Indian fabrics. A Turkish kelim in front of the fire is highlighted by two large Indian lanterns.**

Learning the fresco technique from a Tuscan artisan, Marina mixed four basic hues with water and clay to get the shades she wanted.

The ground floor, once the animals' domain and used for the most part as a stable, has been turned into a huge living and everything-else room, a large kitchen and a dining room – as well as a couple more bedrooms and a bathroom. This is not the conventional way to restore one of these houses, but it is remarkably practical, creating as it does a warm retreat for cold winter days. 'I wanted a natural and comfortable house that was not contrived, where I could gather my thoughts and find myself. I wanted it to look like me, and that is why I combined a traditional, simple countryside style with an Oriental look.'

Marina is a traveller and bought many of the pieces in the house on her journeys around the world. She is particularly attached to the Middle East and India, and has found that Tuscan farmhouse furniture mixes well with country furniture from other worlds. 'There are the 19th-century Chinese peasants' wedding cabinets, the ornamental iron beds I bought in Greece, and the tea tables I found in Turkey.' The carpets too were bought in exotic places such as Syria, Turkey and Tibet after many hours of bargaining over apple tea and shish

kebab. India was the source of most of the textiles – light transparent organza saris, and muslins for curtains and beds; silks for cushions, and linens and raw cottons for the sofas, of which there are several.

'In the decoration of the yellow living room, I was inspired by the caravanserai of Syria. I made long sofas simply from wooden bases along the wall, with big canvas seat cushions and lots more cushions on top.' From Tibet she adapted the nomad tradition of hanging fabric over a door, which adds warmth to the rooms in winter.

Marina likes natural colours and wished to use traditional painting techniques; in typically thorough manner, she learned the fresco technique from a Tuscan artisan and mixed the colour herself, using four basic hues and combining them with water and clay to get the shades she wanted. The main room is ochre; the kitchen/dining room is pink with a green skirting board; the main bedrooms are pale blue; and the iron-bedded room is orange with a grey skirting board. 'These intense, brilliant but natural colours are ideal in a house like this.'

It is interesting to note just how many sources, colours, textiles and styles she has mixed together, her traveller's eye combining as it does Italy, France, Greece, Turkey, Syria, China, India and Tibet, as well as elements from other exotic but as yet unidentified sources.

Above **The unlined sheer curtains are chosen to reinforce the colours of the corridor walls.**

Right **The elaborate 'Pastorale' iron bed in this room dates from the 17th century. Also known as a bishop's bed, it has two curved rods at the foot (with a bar across) designed to hold ceremonial clothing. Low iron pendant lights hang on either side of the bed. Walls the colour of a blood orange, a deep pink Indian bedspread and antique linen complete the picture.**

Left **The pale grey-blue of the roughly finished walls and the gauze bed curtains make this a very feminine room.**

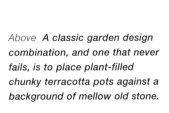
Above **A classic garden design combination, and one that never fails, is to place plant-filled chunky terracotta pots against a background of mellow old stone.**

Right **The pool in the foreground of this tranquil scene was designed to appear to overflow into the landscape beyond, and is bordered by irregularly cut slabs of pinkish-white stone – pietra di Trani *from Puglia. The pool walls have been painted pale pink to echo the colour of the stone, giving an almost translucent cast to the water.**

The natural concept follows through into the garden, where she added to the existing dog roses with many more roses – over 130 varieties, both new and old – as well as lavender, rosemary and other regional species.

The swimming pool, which overlooks the valley, is a tranquil and beautiful spot. 'One summer, I spent two months overseeing every detail; the idea was to choose the widest possible view so that the overflow would seem to vanish into nowhere. As a border for the pool, I chose *pietra di Trani* – large, irregularly cut stones from Puglia, which are whiteish pink. I liked the effect so much that I was persuaded to paint the inside of the pool in the same tone. I didn't know how it would look, of course, but I must say the result is fantastic, and the transparency and colour of the water are truly beautiful.' As indeed is the whole domain.

a double delight

The owners of this 200-year-old house set out to restore it in the manner in which it would originally have been constructed, including laying floors of brick tiles from nearby Impruneta, where pavers are still handmade in the traditional way.

Lori de Mori is an American who, 25 years ago, fell in love with Italy and remains in love to this day. 'I was 19 and studying at UCLA; I went to Florence with a girl friend, promptly fell in love with an Italian, and married him six years later. We travelled regularly between Italy and the US and the desire for a house in Italy grew stronger and stronger. The Florentine architect Andre Benaim, a friend, was also looking for somewhere and we asked him to let us know if he found anything. One day he rang to say that he had indeed found a house, and that it would work for both him and us.

'Andre had said that the house was "in pretty bad shape". At that time, I didn't know what Italians meant by "bad shape", but when I saw the house – with no roof, no windows, and flowers growing through the floor – the phrase seemed to sum it up perfectly.'

Opposite *What was once a dark, light-deprived kitchen is now an airy cooking and eating space displaying the simplicity that is the decorative keynote of the house. The square wooden table beneath the window exemplifies such 'less is more' thinking, surrounded as it is by wooden chairs and a traditional cushioned wooden bench. The flooring is handmade tiles from the nearby town of Impruneta.*

Left *The narrow open hallway connects the main living area with the kitchen end of the house, and from there the main staircase leads directly to the upper floor and the 'ballatoio' between the bedrooms.*

Below *The deep tiled shelf between the sink and the window is ideal for pots of cooking herbs and bulbs.*

When Lori made her first visit to the house, she took her new baby, Julien. By the time the de Moris moved in, Julien was five and had a three-year old sister, Michaela. They decided to stay for a year, and although Lori and her husband later divorced, Lori – having married again, this time to an Englishman – has basically never left.

The property consisted of the original house, a stable attached to the house, and a barn. The house was in the worst condition but was the best situated – houses in this area were always positioned to make the most of the available light, and this one was no exception. 'Andre wanted to move in quickly, so he suggested that we put up half the purchase price and take the house, while he took the stable, which would take less time to restore. He would then draw up the plans and oversee work on the conversion – and we would move in when it was ready. In exchange for this he would get the barn.'

The house had been one that was inhabited on both ground and first floors – unlike in many Italian farmhouses, the animals had been housed in the adjoining barn. 'When I first saw the house, the room

Above **One end of the living area is dominated by an upright piano, all of a piece with the rest of the informal furnishings and atmosphere of the house.**

Right **A narrow hallway links the main living area with the staircase; above it, a landing has been carved out outside**

Michaela de Mori's bedroom and made into a *ballatoio*, a small study space.

Far right **The main bedroom is calm and peaceful beneath the eaves. A broad shelf behind the bed holds pictures and objects, and the column beside the bed is the chimney breast.**

that was then the kitchen was a dark narrow galley, with a wall where the present counter stands. I knew that I wanted one big room. I had become a food writer and my husband at the time was a restaurateur – patently that area was important. We wanted a fireplace placed high enough up the wall to be able to cook in and on, as well being a focal point.'

They were keen to have another large living area where they could eat and sit, and also – in the case of the younger family members – do homework. Upstairs, the plan was for three bedrooms and three bathrooms, one en suite for Lori.

The plans were drawn up and implemented, and – guess what – it works. Andre and family live on one side, and Lori and family on the other. Thanks to Andre, every inch of Lori's house is used. The olive oil is stored under the stairs; there is a minute gallery over the narrow hallway linking the living and eating areas; and, even though the ceilings are not particularly high, there is an all-pervasive feeling of light and air.

Initially, they painted everything white, choosing the colours later. 'We wanted to see how the house came to life. It does seem to me that different places demand different colours that

Left **The bathrooms are decorated and furnished in the same way as the rest of the house – an appealing mixture of the practical and the decorative. This room, in tones of soft white and lit with candles in mirrored sconces, is a sybaritic dream with white ceramic tiles and a shelf for lotions and unguents.**

Opposite and below **White on white – a clever combination of old and new, the basin is set into an old washstand and discreetly plumbed into the wall. An oversized antique mirror is hung above. Carrara marble is much in evidence – luxurious, of course, but far from exotic in this area of Italy, being a local material that is widely used.**

Even though the ceilings are not particularly high, there is an all-pervasive feeling of light and air.

only work there; here it seems to be a warm yellow. There is a lot of wood in the house and soft-toned Carrara marble – an everyday material here. I like things that are handmade with craftsmanship and Italy has wonderful craftsmen and builders.'

Outside, the living is flexible. 'There are three sides to the house, so three places where we can eat according to the seasons and time of day.'

If it sounds perfect, maybe that is because it is. As Lori says, 'After all, I'm based here while my husband is based in London, so I would actually have no reason to be here if I didn't love it so passionately.'

Above **It is hard to believe that this serene façade was once a derelict ruin, roofless, charmless and without an apparent future.**

a house of surprises

La Querciola has all sorts of surprises in store. At first glance, it seems as if it has always been the way it is now. Built in the 17th century, it is obviously a little older than it once was, but seems to be a house that is ageing gracefully. In fact, nothing could be further from the truth.

Above right **In the hallway of La Querciola, a new simple set of stairs by Jean Phillipe Gauvin rises through the centre of the house to connect the lower floor – which used to be cow byres – with the upper living floors.**

Opposite **This narrow sitting room has been decorated by Isabelle with many different motifs and designs. The warm terracotta colour on the walls is embellished with trompe l'oeil garlanded columns and different borders of intricate design.**

When Isabelle and Werner de Borchgrave encountered La Querciola for the first time, it was about as ruined as a house could be. Once the home of some 30 peasants, who lived on the first floor with their cattle ensconced in byres on the ground floor, it was, when they saw it, a derelict house on a rural estate of other, equally derelict houses. It was so derelict in fact that the roof had caved in, crashing through the floors on its way to ground level.

The ambitious plan was to exchange the cows and the workers for four families, including the de Borchgraves. Each family would share the costs of the restoration and then use the place as a summer home. To achieve this end, Werner and Isabelle engaged architect Jean Philippe Gauvin, a man who shared their vision and, with them, was keen to keep the original atmosphere and period of the house –

Left A substantial hall leads off the kitchen, creating an airy open-plan space; painted in a subtle grey, the curves of the arch are highlighted with a darker grey stripe to emphasize the architectural contours.

Right and below Once a shelter for cattle, now a kitchen large enough for everyone, this room has been painted in a soft, subtle colour with bright touches, such as the pink wooden cupboard.

One of the cattle byres has been transformed into a big kitchen, with an oversized table and modern appliances along one wall; the other is a light-filled hall that leads out into a long loggia.

Left **An oversized fireplace, once the hearth around which the original occupants gathered, dominates the upstairs living room. In a subtle combination, bands of yellow and ochre run around the walls. A terracotta tiled floor and a sofa covered in emerald-green linen make the whole room glow with light, and ensure that it is as pleasing in winter as it is in summer.**

Above **In this small bedroom, a delicate, gauzy trompe l'oeil curtain has been painted on the walls. It has been made to look more real by being taken around only a part of the room, and by the fact that in places the wall texture can be seen underneath.**

Right **The upper loggia of the de Borchgrave house is a sanctuary of shaded calm.**

for, as Werner says, 'This type of house imposes on you what it already is; you don't want to intervene too much, and the proportions are so nice that you don't want to change them.'

Like many farmhouses that originally combined both human and animal life, access to the first floor was gained only by external steps, so Gauvin designed a simple, narrow staircase to rise through the centre of the house; this, and the addition of a false light in the ceiling, effectively opened up a previously dead area, adding new space and life to the old building.

On the first floor there were originally five rooms, heated by a large fireplace, where the farmers lived and slept; these were converted into bedrooms, as was space in the attic above,

providing today a grand total of nine bedrooms, each with its own bathroom. The vaulted cow byres on the ground floor were imaginatively converted by Gauvin and now have huge glass doors at either end, which eliminate the difference between outside and in, as well as adding light. One of the byres has been made into a big kitchen, with an oversized table and modern appliances along one wall; the other is a light-filled hall that leads out onto a long loggia.

Although the ground floor is painted white, Isabelle, a noted artist, has hand-painted aspects of many of the rooms. The colours are memorable, and the subtle palette is the result of a happy circumstance. At nearby Arezzo, in the church of San

Right All around the property are discreet and sheltered sitting-out spaces that have been carved out of the original architectural frame.

Below In keeping with the calm atmosphere of the house, the large swimming pool presides serenely over the unspoiled surrounding countryside.

Francesco, a work by Piero della Francesca was being restored with the help of scaffolding; Isabelle was therefore able to see the original colour close-up – 'nose to wall', as Werner says – and the results reflect this detailed observation. Many of the fabrics were also hand-painted by Isabelle – she used a different colour palette in each of the rooms and added cushions that subtly emphasize the scheme. All the furniture was chosen for its suitability in these large spaces: some of it comes from the market at Arezzo, other pieces were originally found in Indonesia. 'Everything had to be big – the scale of the building is huge,' says Werner.

Outside, on a coloured-cement terrace, a long pool gives views over the hills, with a vine-covered pergola to one side; one could ask for little more.

Above and inset **A long loggia runs the length of the house, one end leading to the upper portico; it is perfect space to sit and read, sheltered from the heat of the Tuscan summer sun. Borchgrave fabrics cover the bench and chair.**

a traveller's tale

Much of Gabriella Abbado's working life has been spent in the world of design. She is also an inveterate traveller, absorbing design and ideas wherever she goes, so it is no surprise that her country house in Tuscany is both assured and simple – a confident statement and collection of the pieces and looks that really please her.

Gabriella Abbado's long involvement with design spans both fashion and interiors. During the 1960s she worked with such fashion names as Oleg Cassini and the inimitable Anna Piaggi, and on the interiors side she worked in London in the 1980s with John Howard, designing furniture. All those influences were brought to bear on the restoration and decoration of her Italian country home.

When Gabriella bought the house in 1994, it was, like many buildings of this type, a ruin. Constructed in 1938 on the Engebels' estate, established in 1910, it had originally been a farmhouse for several peasant families, and stood on rough stony ground. 'I restored it, keeping the original structure and proportions, but putting on a new roof and opening up windows that had been filled in, and installing a bathroom – clearly a necessity,' says Gabriella. She wanted to use materials for the restoration

that were sympathetic to the area and the local countryside, materials that were 'solid rather than precious'. Fortunately, she was able to preserve much of the original building materials, although some of the floors had to be replaced.

Gabriella wanted to make the interior comfortable but restrained, which meant preserving its natural simplicity rather than imposing a contrived design-fuelled 'simple look' on what was already there. With hindsight, the house and the owner seem to have been made for each other – certainly in terms of style and taste. Her preference is for honesty in design and architecture, without excessive ornament or unnecessary decoration.

Gabriella has collected 20th-century furniture for many years, and she saw that her new house would be the perfect home for many of the pieces. 'When I saw the quality of the space here, I realized I would be able to use a number of pieces of furniture that I had put in

Above **At one end of the large living room, the fireplace makes a striking focus. On the mantelpiece is a pair of French candlesticks, modelled on the female form. The iron coffee table was designed by Gabriella.**

Right **The library end of the living room features a practical and beautiful table designed by Muramo Palma, which was commissioned by Gabriella in 1974. The low-slung leather chaise longue was designed by Bellini in the early 1970s.**

Opposite **In the master bedroom an antique Tuscan cupboard with its original paint stands next to a Chinese stepladder. On a rug from Morocco is a woven-cane daybed from India.**

Right **Bamboo ladders are used throughout the Abbado home – to hang things from, to reach things, and merely to act as decorative punctuation.**

Below **Even the simplest of bedrooms is full of objects of interest and curiosity, the whole displaying the same happy mix of styles and cultures that is found throughout the house.**

Opposite **Around the wall of the master bedroom a fine grey line has been painted at picture-rail height, separating the lower pale blue pale from the upper pale cream part. The bed is from Kashmir, and Gabriella has added a narrow metal frame between the posts for a linen hanging. Over the bedhead is draped an ornate piece of cutwork linen.**

'I think every house has a colour destiny, which comes from outside – from the local history, the setting and landscape, to the variety of light throughout the day.'

store and that were part of a past that was dear to me; they were all of a style popular in the 1970s and of course I chose pieces suitable for a country house.'

The result is an extraordinary success. Solid, chunky pieces of furniture fill the rooms and emphasize the basic architecture, the curved arches, the heavy beams. There are also many decorative objects and works of art from Africa and Asia, because Gabriella loves the forms found in the artistic expression of those cultures.

Throughout the house is colour, chosen in an artistic and unusual way. Gabriella's understanding of colour is no doubt influenced and honed by her years spent working in both interior and fashion design. She sees it as a genuinely organic part of any space, not just as a device used to brighten or highlight a given area, but as an almost elemental part of the whole, and chosen not by chance or personal whim, but almost because there is no alternative.

'I think that every house has a colour destiny, which comes from outside – from the local history, the setting and landscape, to the variety of light throughout the day. The strong colours reflect my personality, but they

Right **In the master bathroom basins set into a wooden top are lit with Art Deco lamps dating – like the wooden mirror frame – from the 1930s. On either side of the mirror are groups of tiles from Seville.**

Below **This simple, immensely well-designed shower room incorporates a slatted wooden base, built-in storage and a shower head attached to the wall. Bands of painted colour add further decorative interest.**

also correspond to the relative harshness of the countryside.' Much of the colour comes in shots supplied through textiles found on her travels. 'From the simplest to the most luxurious, textiles always have a story to tell.' In another departure from the conventional, the house changes its look according to the time of year, for Gabriella believes that a living environment should renew itself with the seasons, and that colours and fabrics should be rich and warm in winter, cool and simple in summer. 'Fabrics and light determine the balance of the interior decoration,' she says. 'As a consequence, my homes have a series of "outfits" depending on the seasons. You could say that the house has its own wardrobe.'

Left **A sun-drenched terrace leads onto a grassed area with wide views of the landscape beyond. Although protected by a wall, it nevertheless remains within the wider countryside, while at the same time seeming very much part of the house rather than an extension.**

Above and below **Built in the mid-20th century, the house – a former home for several families of peasants who worked on the estate – needed a roof and various essential additions. The setting and the landscape were the departure points for the interior and exterior decoration.**

revival of a stronghold

Over its 800-year-life, Castel Ruggero, in the Chianti region, has been through several different incarnations. Built in the 13th century as a monastery, where wine was made, it was turned into a fortified castle in the 15th century. By the time the family of artist Camilla d'Afflitto, the present owner, bought it, some centuries later, the need for fortified buildings was past, and Camilla and her sisters grew up there in tranquillity.

When Camilla inherited Castel Ruggero in 2001, she wanted to make changes to the interior. Every generation has its own way of living, and to her the house seemed oppressive and dark. Her desire was, she says, 'to return life to the house in a way that reflects my own artistic and living experience'. So she embarked on extensive restorations – and the end result was restorative rather than reconstructive, for the castle building remains entirely original, as it always has been, and the work has been of renewal rather than replacement, of burnishing rather than bashing.

Camilla decided not to alter in any significant way the layout of the two floors. On the ground floor there are two living rooms, one larger than the other, and what was a billiard room is now

Above left The house's exterior has changed little over the years, through its incarnations from wine-producing monastery to fortified castle to family home.

Above In this mix of classical taste and retro chic, a circular table has been covered with a traditional cloth, and a collection of Capo di Monte ceramics and offbeat floral displays is lit by a modern lamp designed by Roberto Gerosa.

Right A long hallway is used as an additional living room and furnished with a quantity of comfortable chairs and sofas, upholstered with imaginative flair, for the use of Ruggero's many guests. The lamps and wall lights are again by Gerosa.

used as an occasional dining room. Next to the dining area is a room that was once blocked off, but which she has re-opened and turned into a kitchen. Upstairs on the first floor there is a further sitting room, a study and eight bedrooms, each with its own bathroom.

Throughout the house, the original floors have been retained, and these form the underpinning for the whole decorative approach. As Camilla says, 'The original floors are one of the most beautiful features of the house, both in terms of their colour and patina, as well as the warmth they create in every room.'

With this solid architectural and decorative foundation as a starting point, Camilla could map out a route towards her objective, which had always been to combine the

Above **Part of the charm of the house lies in the heavy carved wooden doors, and Camilla has wisely chosen to emphasize them by simplifying the rest of the space and using only a few carefully placed pieces of furniture and objects.**

Left **The winter sitting room: Camilla has covered the 1950s chairs and sofa with witty mixtures of silks and velvets. The antique Persian rug, from which the furnishing colours were taken, belonged to her Turkish grandfather. The floor lamp is by Roberto Gerosa, and a lamp with a Venini glass base sits on the table.**

traditional furniture of her childhood with her own collections of both decorative art and textiles. She began by taking stock of the existing furniture; she decided to sell the heavier and more ponderous pieces, and at the same time cleared the rooms of all the existing decorative objects, putting them into cupboards to be re-evaluated and reintroduced over time in different contexts. 'In this way, I have achieved a harmony between my past and my present – and the soul of the house continues to grow and change,' she says.

Then came the moment for Camilla to introduce her own collections – particularly her collection of Italian vases, which she had begun to put together while she was in her twenties. She also possesses a large and varied collection of textiles, which she has collected all her life, and which includes Italian, American and Oriental pieces. All these she has placed around the house, combining West with East and old with new in a completely original way.

Above **The hallway outside the bathroom has been painted in shades of blue running through to grey, applied in broad horizontal stripes. The tiled floor – which is original, like all the floors in the house – is part of the decorative scheme.**

Right **Once the girls' bathroom, this room was decorated in the 1950s by Camilla's mother and still retains its charming flowery wallpaper. Camilla has painted the dressing table and chair to tone with the original scheme.**

The architect and decorator Roberto Gerosa has contributed enormously to the restoration project at Castel Ruggero, adding lamps and sofas, and introducing colour contrasts and combinations that are witty and eccentric.

The outcome is a unique house that manages to be both serious and quirky at the same time, with something interesting or unusual to look at around every corner. 'I don't enjoy the dark, lifeless, boring interiors that you sometimes find in Italian country houses,' says Camilla. 'I have tried to create a home which is the antithesis of that style – a home that reflects my love and passion for colour and light, as well as illustrating my respect for all the artists whose work is represented throughout the house.'

Opposite **The emerald tiles in this bathroom are the original mosaic tiles from the 1950s.**

Above and inset **The master bedroom has a bedspread in silk from Scalamandre. A 1950s chair has been covered with a cotton fabric from the same period. Above the long line of fitted wardrobes is a collection of 1950s ceramics.**

This page **As befits a castle of such long standing, the formal gardens with tight, box-edged beds, clipped and nurtured over many hundreds of years, provide a suitable foreground to the unadorned façade.**

photography credits

All photographs by Chris Tubbs.   **key**: **a**=above, **b**=below, **r**=right, **l**=left, **c**=centre.

Endpapers Giorgio and Ilaria Miani's Podere Casellacce in Val d'Orcia; **page 1** a house in Tuscany planned and decorated by architect Piero Castellini; **2–3** Giorgio and Ilaria Miani's Podere Casellacce in Val d'Orcia; **4** a house in Maremma, Tuscany designed by Contemporanea; **5** Casa Colonica in Tuscany – interior design Isabelle de Borchgrave, architect Jean Philippe Gauvin; **6–7** Antica Casa Le Rondini, the home of 'green' architect Carlo Meacci and Fulvia Musso; **8–9** a house in Tuscany planned and decorated by architect Piero Castellini; **10–11** Brogino; **12al** Toia Saibene and Giuliana Magnifico's home in Lucignano, Tuscany; **12b** Vanni and Nicoletta Calamai's home near Siena; **12–13a** Antica Casa Le Rondini, the home of 'green' architect Carlo Meacci and Fulvia Musso; **13b** Brogino; **13ar** Prato di Sotto in Umbria designed and restored by Penny Radford; **14–21** Toia Saibene and Giuliana Magnifico's home in Lucignano, Tuscany; **22–29** Prato di Sotto in Umbria designed and restored by Penny Radford; **30–37** Brogino; **38–45** Vanni and Nicoletta Calamai's home near Siena; **46–53** Antica Casa Le Rondini, the home of 'green' architect Carlo Meacci and Fulvia Musso; **54–56** Mimmi O'Connell's home in Tuscany; **57** Giorgio and Ilaria Miani's Podere Casellacce in Val d'Orcia; **58–63** Sebastian Abbado's 'I Falchi' in Val d'Orcia; **64–71** a house in Maremma, Tuscany designed by Contemporanea; **72–81** Giorgio and Ilaria Miani's Podere Casellacce in Val d'Orcia; **82–89** Mimmi O'Connell's home in Tuscany; **90–91** a house in Tuscany planned and decorated by architect Piero Castellini; **92al** and **92–93a** Podere Porrona, a private country home between Val d'Orcia and Val di Chiana in Tuscany; **92bl and 93ar** a house in Tuscany planned and decorated by architect Piero Castellini; **92–93b** Giorgio and Ilaria Miani's Podere Buon Riposo in Val d'Orcia; **94–103** Simone de Looze's home in Tuscany, Le Porciglia; **104–11** a house in Tuscany planned and decorated by architect Piero Castellini; **112–19** Podere Porrona, a private country home between Val d'Orcia and Val di Chiana in Tuscany; **120–31** Giorgio and Ilaria Miani's Podere Buon Riposo in Val d'Orcia; **132–39** a house in Tuscany planned and decorated by architect Piero Castellini; **140–41** Casa Colonica in Tuscany – interior design Isabelle de Borchgrave, architect Jean Philippe Gauvin; **142l&ar** artist Camilla d'Afflitto's home in Tuscany and studio for her paintings, architect and interior decorator Roberto Gerosa; **142br** Marina Ferrara Pignatelli's home in Val d'Orcia, Tuscany; **143l** artist Camilla d'Afflitto's home in Tuscany and studio for her paintings, architect and interior decorator Roberto Gerosa; **143r** Marina Ferrara Pignatelli's home in Val d'Orcia, Tuscany; **144–53** Marina Ferrara Pignatelli's home in Val d'Orcia, Tuscany; **154–61** Podere Sala, Lori de Mori's home in Tuscany restored by architect André Benaim; **162–69** Casa Colonica in Tuscany – interior design Isabelle de Borchgrave, architect Jean Philippe Gauvin; **170–77** Gabriella Cantaluppi Abbado's home in Monticchiello; **178–87** artist Camilla d'Afflitto's home in Tuscany and studio for her paintings, architect and interior decorator Roberto Gerosa.

business credits

architects, designers and properties featured in this book

André Benaim

Architect (restoration and new build) and theatre set designer

Studio Architettura Benaim
Via Giotto 37
50121 Florence
Italy
tel + 39 055 6632 84
fax + 39 055 6726 15

benaim@tin.it

Pages 154–61.

Antica Casa Le Rondini

Bed and breakfast

Via M. Pierucci nr. 21
Colle di Buggiano
Pistoia
Italy
tel + 39 0572 33313
fax + 39 0572 905361

www.anticacasa.it
info@anticacasa.it

Pages 6–7, 12–13a, 46–53.

Brogino

Brogino is available to rent from Invitation to Tuscany

www.invitationtotuscany.co.uk

Pages 10–11, 13b, 30–37.

Camilla d'Afflitto

Via di Castel Ruggero 33
50012 Bagno a Ripoli (FI)
Italy
tel + 39 055 64 99 237/222
Pages 142l, 142ar, 143l, 178–87.

Contemporanea

Vicolo del Babuino 8
00187 Rome
Italy
tel + 39 6 3233465
fax + 39 6 32502828

contemporaneasrl@libero.it

Pages 4, 64–71.

Gabriella Abbado

Designer

tel + 39 333 90 30 809
Pages 170–77.

Ilaria Miani

Shop

Via Monserrato 35
00186 Rome
Italy
tel + 39 0668 33160
ilariamiani@tin.it

Podere Casellacce and Podere Buon Riposo in Val d'Orcia are available for rent

Pages 2–3, 57, 72–81, 92–93b, 120–31, endpapers.

Isabelle de Borchgrave

Interior design

52 rue Gachard
B–1050 Brussels
Belgium
tel + 32 (0)2 648 53 50
werner@isabelle-de-borchgrave.be
La_querciola@yahoo.fr
Also involved in this project:

Jean Philippe Gauvin

Architect

40 Ter avenue de Suffren
Paris 75015
France
jp.gauvin@bracqgauvin.com
Pages 5, 140–41, 162–69.

Mimmi O'Connell

Design consultant

Port of Call Ltd
19 Ensor Mews
London SW7 3BT
tel 020 7589 4836
fax 020 7823 9828

moconnell@portofcall.co.uk

For information on renting La Scuola, call our London office.

Pages 54–56, 82–89.

Paola Navone

Architect and designer

OTTO SRL
Corso San Gottardo 22
20136 Milan
Italy
tel + 39 02 58104926
fax + 39 02 58112397

paola.navone@paolanavone.it
Also involved in this project:

Peter Curzon

Landscape architect

petercurzon@mailtrust.it
Pages 92al, 92–93a, 112–19.

Penny Radford

Design, restoration and project management

Prato di Sotto
Santa Giuliana
06015 Pierantonio (PG)
Italy
tel + 39 075 941 73 83
fax + 39 075 941 24 73
www.umbriaholidays.com
pennyradford@libero.it

Pages 13ar, 22–29.

Piero Castellini

Architect

Via della Rocca 5
Milan
Italy
tel + 39 02 48005384

studiocastellini@libero.it

Pages 1, 8–9, 90–91, 92bl, 93ar, 104–11, 132–39.

Sebastian Abbado

Project developer–architectural design, urban reconstruction and landscaping

tel 07899 790459
Also involved in this project:

Luigi Vivarelli

Bed metal worker

tel + 39 578 758 728
mobile + 39 347 391 9911

Benedetta Brunotti

tel + 39 34769 78768

Lorenzo Capaccio

tel + 39 34977 97928
Pages 58–63.

Simone de Looze

Interiors

tel + 39 335 572 06 85
akadelooze@inwind.it
Also involved in this project:

Anthony Collett

Collett Zarzycki Ltd
Fernhead Studios
2b Fernhead Road
London W9 3ET
tel 020 8969 6967
fax 020 8960 6480

www.collett-zarzycki.com

Pages 94–103.

index

Page numbers in italics refer to captions.

acknowledgments

The publishers would like to thank all those who allowed us to photograph their homes and who made us so welcome throughout each shoot. Particular thanks are due to Penny Radford and to Carlo Meacci and Fulvia Musso for their kindness in allowing us to stay with them while photographing their homes.